THE TRINITY RIVER

Photographs by Luther Smith

THE TRINITY RIVER

Photographs by Luther Smith

Essays by Mike Nichols
and
Thomas W. Southall

TCU PRESS

Fort Worth

Smith, Luther
    The Trinity River / photographs by Luther Smith ; essays by Mike Nichols and
Thomas W. Southall.
        p. cm.
    ISBN 0-87565-168-2 (pbk. : alk. paper)
    1. Trinity River (Tex.)—Pictorial works. 2. Trinity River (Tex.)—Description and
travel. 3. Landscape—Texas—Trinity River Region—Pictorial works. 4.
Landscape photography—Texas—Trinity River Region. I. Nichols, Mike, 1949-   .
II. Southall, Thomas, 1951-   . III. Title.
F392. T83S65   1997
976. 4—dc21
                                                                                    97-318
                                                                                    CIP

The photographs in this volume were made with support from the
TCU Research and Creative Activities Fund.

Publication of this book was made possible in part by generous grants from the
Helen Irwin Littauer Educational Trust and from Mrs. Ruth May.

Design by Shadetree Studio
Printed in Hong Kong

To my loving wife, Pat

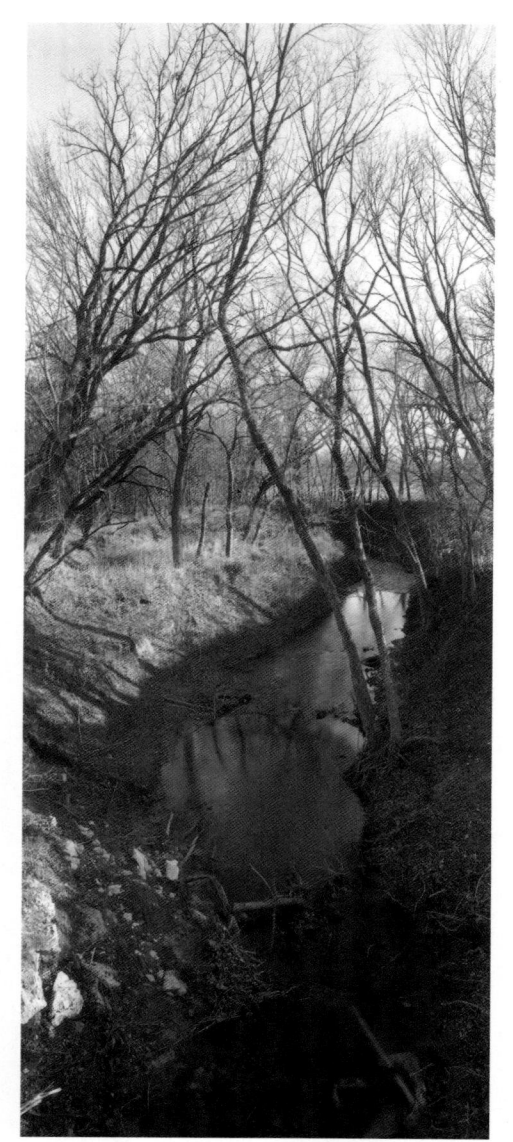

Contents

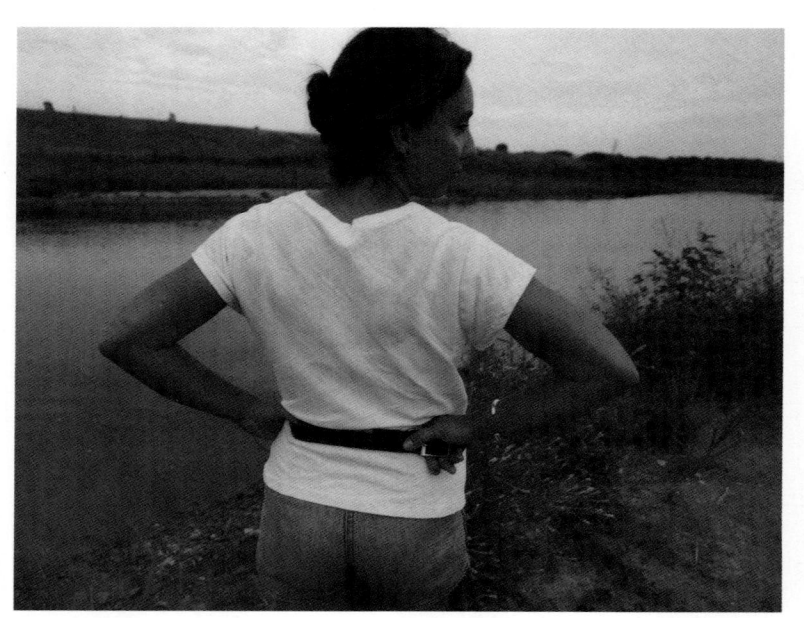

Preface

When we first moved to Fort Worth in 1983, my wife, Pat, and I started taking walks along the West Fork of the Trinity River. We live on the hill north of downtown, in the bend created by the West Fork as it flows past Rockwood Park, is joined by the Clear Fork, then moves past the stockyards.

The banks and levee of the channeled river were then an undeveloped park where few other people seemed to venture. Occasionally we would see a fisherman, but mostly it was us and the dogs, Mishwa and Chadow. The dogs liked running along the river chasing whatever was available. I liked the green space, liked being in the country, except the downtown skyline was nearby.

In 1986 I began serious landscape photography. I started by imagining how to photograph the landscape as I drove through it, making imaginary pictures. I would look for the best point of view as I drove and watch how different types of light changed the way the landscape looked. Although not naturally a morning person, I found myself getting up in the dark, hours before sunrise, to load the truck and drive an hour or more to the place I wanted to photograph. I wanted to be there before the sun came up, so that I could capture the early light.

I purchased a large-format 8" x 10" camera, the traditional camera for landscape photography. It produced the kind of photographs I was looking for—detailed, with a wealth of tonal beauty, rivaling the complex beauty of the landscape. Later I purchased an antique 7" x 17" panoramic or banquet view camera, used from the turn of the century to the 1940s to photograph groups.

Using these view cameras allowed me to slow down and experience the landscape. With the camera on a tripod, I could compose the picture carefully, spending an hour or more at each scene looking, thinking, and organizing the image. The view camera allows the photographer to control the look of a picture, even controlling the rise and fall of the horizon.

At first, I didn't know the Trinity River photographs were a series. I simply selected sites without a theme in mind. I photographed what interested me and what I thought might make a good photograph. Later, I organized the images that seemed to go together into groups. The Trinity River series began this way.

Soon I was exploring more of the river. In the 1990-1991 academic year, I was on sabbatical leave from TCU and had a TCU Research and Creative Activities Fund grant to develop the river

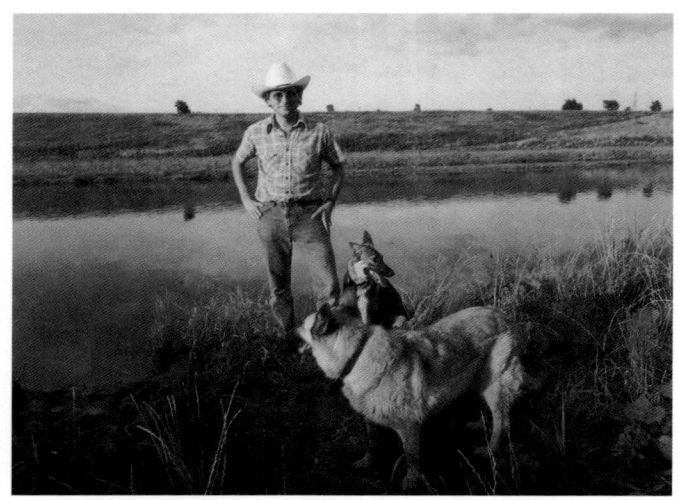

series. Most of these photographs were made during that time.

Consulting a detailed map, I tried to cross the river at every possible point from the edges of the basin, where the branches are small, to the I-10 crossing east of Houston, near Wallisville, where the river empties into Trinity Bay, headed for Galveston Bay and the Gulf of Mexico.

My idea was to produce a compelling body of work that would contribute to an understanding of the environment and would also challenge the viewer's sense of photography. But first, the photographs had to stand on their own as images. Each has to tell me a story.

The act of making photographs at its best is an act of grace. The photographer simply prepares through discipline for the gift.

—Luther Smith
Texas Christian University
September 1996

The Trinity River

Mike Nichols

. . . the river is a strong brown god—
sullen, untamed and intractable.
T. S. Eliot

It lacks the length of the Amazon, the white-water rapids of the Colorado, the history of the Nile. Nevertheless, it is a shaper of destinies.

It is the Trinity River, and if you follow its course as it meanders through seventeen counties in North Texas, you will pass five million people who are where they are because the Trinity is where it is.

For hundreds, even thousands, of years—a drop in the bucket in terms of Trinity time—the river has attracted people and so shaped their destiny. Dust its banks for fingerprints and you would find those of prehistoric cultures, Native Americans, horse soldiers, outlaws, hoboes, sharecroppers, dreamers, millionaires, and the middle class.

The first people to settle along the river were attracted to it because it offered cheap transportation and good water to drink and to power mills, to water cattle, and to irrigate crops. Certainly the river was a big reason why Fort Worth and Dallas were settled where they were 150 years ago. And those cities have continued to attract people long after the river no longer does. And even though for most of us today the Trinity plays no part in any decision to live here in its watershed area, we live here because our parents lived here because their parents lived here.

And millions more not born to the Trinity have moved to it. A person from Manhattan, New York, or Manhattan, Kansas, might relocate to Fort Worth or Dallas to take a job in electronics or banking. But that job is here because the cities are here because the river is here.

Thus with divine impartiality the Trinity—the strong brown god—has shaped the destiny of all of us who live in its watershed.

Even the name bespeaks a deity. The river was named *La Santissima de la Trinidad* by Spanish General Alonzo de León more than three hundred years ago—named for the feast day of the Holy Trinity.

De León saw the river near its mouth at the Gulf of Mexico. He was hundreds of miles from its sources. For indeed the Trinity has not one but four sources. And for a shaper of destinies, the Trinity

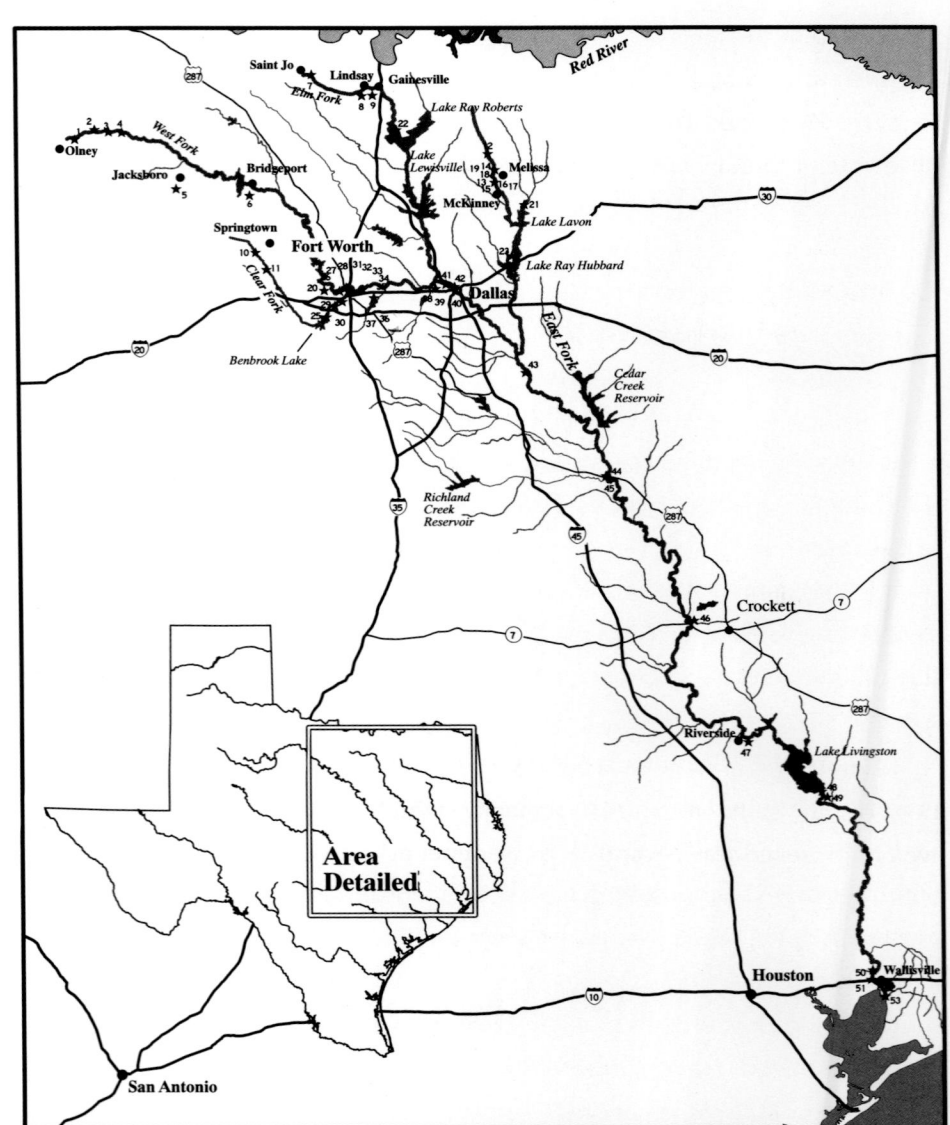

Stars refer to photographs by number

has humble sources, such as the unmarked and unremarkable gully near McMurtry Road in Archer County. That gully is the headwater of the West Fork. The river has three other forks, each with a headwater as humble: the East Fork begins in Grayson County, the Elm Fork in Montague County, and the Clear Fork in Parker County. The Clear Fork merges with the West Fork near downtown Fort Worth. The Elm Fork merges with the West Fork near downtown Dallas; at that junction the Trinity River formally begins. Further south, the East Fork merges with the main river. Those four forks form a river that has the most populated basin in Texas.

As surely as the Trinity connects people, it also connects places. Its four forks form a river that—fed by hundreds of creeks that are, in turn, fed by thousands of anonymous gullies and bar ditches and springs—drains eighteen thousand square miles. Each fork, each bar ditch, each spring contributes to the main river. Thus the Trinity is an organic Internet: it connects every place to every other place as it flows 550 miles through Texas, ultimately emptying into the Gulf of Mexico near Galveston. A drop of rain that falls in Megargel or Tioga or Cayuga has a chance to someday swim free in the Gulf and even in the seven seas beyond. A grasshopper at the edge of Ten-Mile Creek or Eagle Mountain Lake that leaps before it looks in April may well feed a fish in the Atlantic come September.

The Trinity obeys only one law: gravity. In Archer County, at the headwater of the West Fork, the Trinity is about one thousand feet above sea level; at Dallas County, it has fallen to about five hundred feet. By the time it flows into Walker County, it is less than two hundred feet and sloping toward sea level. Likewise, each raindrop that falls on a tree in the river's watershed drips from upper leaf to lower leaf, each trickle flows from the gully on a hill to the gully in a valley, riding the gravity express to the Trinity and on to the Gulf.

Along its course through Texas, the Trinity sometimes slinks, sometimes struts. It passes through prairie, timberlands, and marshes, through red sand, brown clay, and black gumbo. It flows past rickety tin-topped wooden barns that lean in italics and past glass-and-steel skyscrapers that are temples to verticality. It flows past fields that yield beef and oil—the meat and mythos of Texas.

But the Trinity is not always beautiful. Its creeks may be little more than watering holes, their muddy bottoms dotted with the hoofprints of cattle in a sort of bovine pointillism. During Texas droughts, its ponds can be dry, containing only the rumor of water. Its bridges are used as bulletin boards, spray-painted with graffiti and lovers' initials. In stretches the river is lined with litter—the flotsam of our conspicuous consumption.

But other stretches of the river—thanks, in part, to conservation efforts—are natural and unspoiled. Wildlife thrives. Herons walk on stilts. Raccoons wear masks and break into mussel shells. Trees on each side of the river bend their branches over the water, as if reaching across to hold hands.

In one place, the river is fast-flowing and glittering where the glare of the sun turns it to quicksilver; in another place, it is sluggish and chocolate brown. At times it seems almost inert. But then the wind comes sashaying down from the Panhandle or up from the Gulf and raises goose bumps on the surface.

Like most rivers, the Trinity has been all things to all people: highway and playground, supermarket and landfill, swimming hole and laundry, burial ground, bathtub, baptismal font, and sewer. We have dredged it, diverted it, polluted it, bridged it, even —like John Neely Bryan—dreamed of navigating it.

When Bryan founded the settlement of Dallas at a white-rock crossing on the Trinity in 1841, he hoped that the river could be navigated, making Dallas a landlocked seaport. Bryan dreamed of making the river navigable to Galveston. He envisioned steamboats plying back and forth, carrying passengers and goods such as cotton, cowhides, and timber. The Trinity would be Dallas' river-road to the world.

Another early proponent of Trinity navigation in the mid-1800s concurred, forecasting that within a decade "the citizens of the Red River counties will find it more advantageous to direct their trade to Galveston by the Trinity than to continue it by the Red River to New Orleans."

Such proponents of navigation saw the river as a cheap alternative to railroads, which often charged high freight rates. And so for more than a century successive generations chased Bryan's dream, campaigning for government and community support for navigation between Dallas and Galveston. They formed committees, they raised funds, they lobbied congresses on behalf of their river. Men and their machines dredged it, channeled it, even changed its course.

Docks and turning basins and a series of locks and dams were envisioned, efforts were made to clear out snags, drifts, and debris from the river. But only a few times did steamboats complete the trip between Dallas and Galveston. And even then, the voyage took weeks and even months. Each time logs and trees had to be cleared, sections of bridges had to be removed or temporarily held up by enthusiastic crowds using crowbars so that the boat could pass under.

Despite the zeal of proponents, 150 years later Bryan's dream remains just that.

During those 150 years we have not always been kind to the Trinity. In particular, during the last half of the twentieth century inadequately treated wastewater has polluted the river. Bacteria that thrive on organic matter in the water depleted its oxygen level, resulting in massive fish kills. But in recent years heightened environmental awareness has led to laws to clean up the river and monitor its water quality. As a result, pollution has decreased. The river has even been stocked with trout in places.

The quality of water in the Trinity affects more than the fish. Today twenty-nine lakes along the river supply drinking water to people in its watershed. Thus the Trinity retains its importance; its ebb and flow remain the pulse of North Texas. Water from the lakes is piped to homes and businesses, then drained to wastewater treatment plants, where it is treated and returned to the river—recycling at its best.

During the hot, dry months of the Texas summer, when evaporation exceeds precipitation and the river would otherwise be low from lack of rainfall, more than ninety percent of the water in stretches of the Trinity is supplied by treatment plants. Such recycling will become even more important in the future. Our need for water is predicted to double over the next fifty years, making the Trinity twice as vital.

The lakes and their dams, too, have helped to regulate the Trinity's level, which, because the river is fed solely by rainfall, drops during dry seasons and rises perilously during wet seasons.

But our attempts to tame the Trinity also have created an ironic, vicious cycle. As we channel the river and build levees along its banks to prevent flooding, such improvements allow more development along the river: We build homes and businesses, and with them we build foundations, parking lots, streets, and driveways whose impervious surfaces prevent rain from soaking into the ground. Instead the rain drains into storm-sewer systems and ultimately pours into the river, making it more prone to flooding. The process is repeated when we build reservoirs along the river. Around those reservoirs we then build vacation homes and lake resorts and streets, creating more runoff that is diverted into the river, again making it more prone to flooding.

Today the emphasis of the Environmental Protection Agency, the Army Corps of Engineers, and other federal and states agencies concerned with land use for rivers such as the Trinity has shifted to a policy of "multi-objective river corridor development." That means developing a river corridor for as many compatible, benign uses as possible—uses such as flood plain and storm water management, wildlife habitat, recreation, greenways, alternative transportation routes, location of utility and communication lines, and even commercial development.

Such attention is well timed. Because as each generation has moved further away from direct contact with the land, we have had less reason to pay attention to the Trinity. For most of us most of the time, the river is a vague geographic feature that we cross at North Main in Fort Worth or at the Houston Street viaduct in Dallas. We are aware of the Trinity only occasionally—when it gives us pain.

It gives us pain when it floods. In recent years, levees have lessened the danger of flooding, but certainly three generations know the story—now part of our urban folklore—of how high the Trinity floodwaters rose at the Montgomery Ward store on Seventh Street in Fort Worth in May 1949. Eleven people died; Fort Worth suffered $11 million in property damage. In another May—of 1908 —in Dallas the river flooded downtown buildings, railroad tracks, and the central power plant, and left four thousand homeless. At such times the Trinity seems like a god, omnipotent and wrathful. Millions of dollars worth of property are lost. People are drowned. And when they drown, they are just as dead as if they had drowned in the Mississippi, the Amazon, or the Nile.

The Trinity River is at once unnoticed and undeniable.

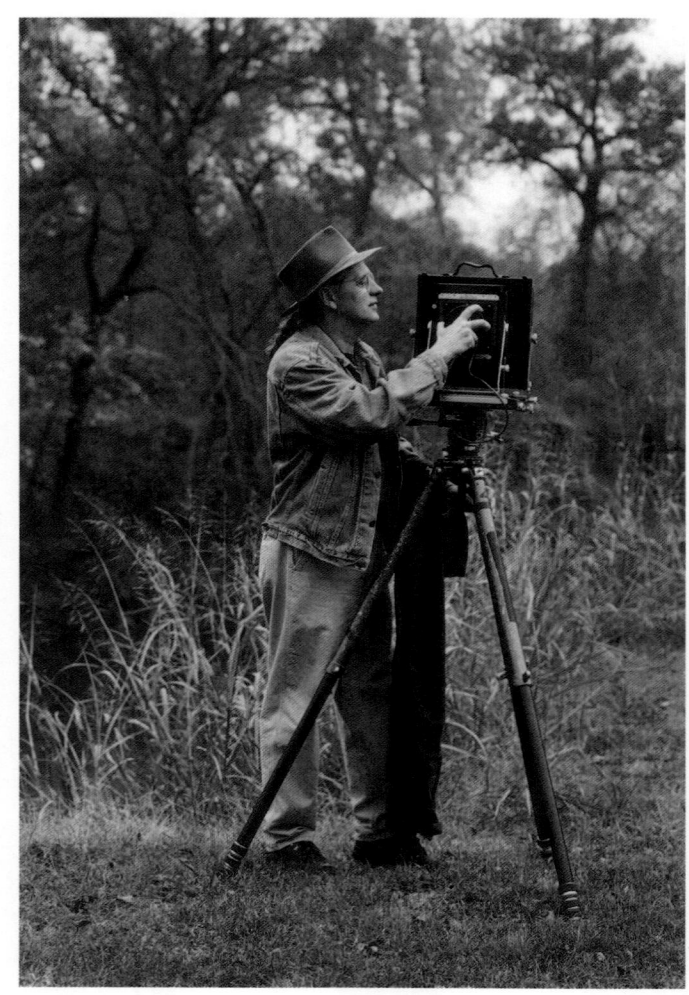

Reflections on a River's Convergence

Thomas W. Southall

Luther Smith's photographs of the Trinity River are as modest and unpretentious as the river itself. Lacking scenes of dramatic canyons and rapids or bustling docks and ports, his images of the river banks might at first seem repetitive studies of undistinguished, unpopulated landscapes. But after repeated viewing, the distinctive character and quality of the river unfold for us, much as they slowly did for Smith as his photographic project progressed. Like Henry David Thoreau in his careful observations at Walden Pond, we become aware of the beauty in the unrecognized details of nature like twisted interlocking branches of young saplings, scrubby dry brush along the western forks of the river compared to the luxuriant ground cover and foliage of the Fort Worth greenway, which benefits from the convergence of the tributaries in the metropolitan area. We see the decayed skull of a dead dog as a kind of *memento mori* along the neglected banks, and we become especially aware of the ever-present effects of man, even though people are seldom seen. Even the seemingly benign character of the river is contradicted by Smith's views of the occasional flooding that suggest that the apparent calm of the river should not be mistaken for docility or powerlessness.

Smith's photographs and his interest in the river are not about power and drama but about subtlety and contemplation, about one man's experience of a neglected river. Rather than an environmental diatribe about nature and mankind's responsibility in general, Smith's photographs are about a personal, individual experience and understanding of the river. By sharing the way the secrets of this subtle landscape have been revealed to him, Smith helps us see, understand, and value commonplace landscapes such as the Trinity that have been ignored and abused for too long.

Smith, like so many of us, is a Texas transplant. With no family roots or extensive experience in the state, he had little interest in the Texas landscape prior to his arrival to teach photography at Texas Christian University in 1983. His childhood was spent on a farm in Mississippi and later in Illinois, but his adult life was far more urban. During college at the University of Illinois at Champaign/Urbana he began to photograph seriously, although he didn't pursue an art major.

He went on to concentrate on photography on the graduate level at the Rhode Island School of Design, where he studied with

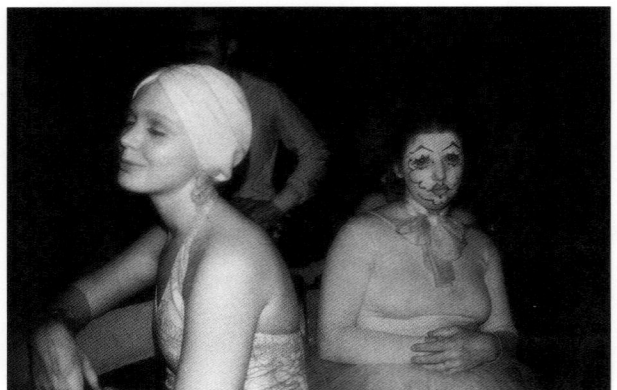

Harry Callahan, Aaron Siskind, and others. His most extensive photographic campaign at RISD captured animated party and bar scenes using grainy 35mm infrared film, closer to the documentary style of Garry Winogrand than to the refined, formal view-camera studies of his RISD mentors. When he returned to the University of Illinois to teach in 1974, he continued this style of "street documentary" with a series on high school students.

When Smith came to Texas he found ripe new material to continue his exploration of the rituals and tribulations of young high school students in the specialized and characteristically Texan scene of teenage rodeo. Smith was drawn to the energy and character of these adolescents much as earlier photographers Geoff Winningham, Garry Winogrand, and Elliott Erwitt had followed the singular Texas extremes of professional wrestling, high school football, cheerleading, and livestock shows.

Smith's people-oriented, energetic, and angst-ridden images of bars, parties, and adolescent maturation rites might seem about as far as can be imagined from these contemplative, usually unpopular Trinity River landscapes. A close friend and fellow RISD graduate, Peter Fereseten, known for his passionate social documentation of Fort Worth's minority cultures, even accused Smith of going soft because he was turning toward seemingly less dynamic, less socially concerned, and more easily accessible subject matter. Closer examination, however, reveals that Smith's photographic explorations of seemingly typical teenagers and conventional landscapes actually have a lot in common by drawing attention to normally unnoticed qualities that give a distinctive character to this place and region. While natives and long-time Texas residents may become desensitized to commonplace subjects and scenes, Smith's position as a newcomer helped make him observant of and sensitive to the singular qualities of such diverse subjects as teenage rodeo and riverside landscapes. As his Trinity River project progressed, it became a different way for Smith to explore many themes first suggested in his rodeo series: identity, hopes, aspirations, bravado, truth, posturing, and performance. It is a sad commentary that our communities' negligent attitudes toward nature and our immediate environment could so easily find parallels in the behavioral patterns of teenagers.

Smith's initial series of river photographs was made primarily around Fort Worth. Among his earliest images of the river was a 1987 panoramic night view from the river's bank looking toward downtown, depicting the bright lights of Fort Worth's tall downtown buildings rising like some Las Vegas Prometheus from the barren landscape. More telling and anticipatory of the less dramatic, more contemplative work that was to come was his decision to return during the quieter, more subtle moments of the day, when the skyline was less dramatic but more in harmony with the landscape. Unlike the ironic night view of conflicting contrasts between nature and man's constructions, Smith's day view is a little like the emperor's clothes, showing the city laid bare without the glamorous pretensions or disguises of the night. While the daytime image is quieter and less conventionally beau-

tiful, the buildings actually seem more integrated into the landscape. The results may be contrary to the contrasting drama that the builders and designers had intended, but celebration of the commonplace, not artificial drama, is at the heart of Smith's work.

After photographing the river near Fort Worth, Smith was inspired to branch out to the dramatic rechanneling of the river through Dallas and also to go upstream to examine the four primary forks, where the river is barely a trickle. He also expanded his study by showing the river under flood and various seasonal conditions. The expansion of the subject, however, should be not mistaken for an attempt to make a history of the river and its varying character and properties.

Neither a documentary history of the river nor a narrative of its changing character as it meanders through different regions, this book follows the general progression of the river from its four forks through their convergence in the Metroplex and beyond, but there is no attempt to consider its different facets for a comprehensive scientific or historical document. Readers might expect to find a linear narrative following the river's progression, like the great literary river narratives by Twain, or the documentary narrative presented in Laura Gilpin's photographic book, *The Rio Grande: River of Destiny* (1947), which traces the river's progression through divergent cultures and geography from its sources high in the Colorado Rockies, through the varied landscape and contrasting Pueblo, Hispanic, and Anglo cultures of New Mexico until Gilpin shows it finally emptying into the Gulf of Mexico in a triumphant crescendo of light reflecting off its winding surface.

But the quiet Trinity is hardly to be mistaken for the mighty Mississippi, nor even the dry but dramatic Rio Grande. If there is a story to Smith's work, it is not the linear progress of an increasingly powerful river but the modest and undramatic convergence of the river's four small forks in the Fort Worth and Dallas Metroplex. The distinctive character of the Trinity may be that it lacks the simplistic linear quality we expect of a river system. As both a map and Smith's photographs show, the Trinity is a complex, hard-to-follow network of tributaries of varying importance and flow. The defining pattern is less like the roots of an increasingly grand tree trunk than a meandering web converging in the Metroplex. The development of Smith's project, first with an interest in the river's passage through Fort Worth, then slowly working outward, up and down the river, is in keeping with the distinctive character of the river itself. By refusing to impose either artificial drama or simplistic logic on a hard-to-define river system, Smith's photographs remain faithful to the spirit of their subject.

Smith's photographs make us aware of the need to value and preserve even the most seemingly commonplace landscape, not just America's most spectacular scenery such as Yosemite and the Grand Canyon, which we have turned into national parks for people to "visit" nature. As numerous commentators — photographer Robert Adams and naturalist Barry Lopez among them —

have observed, there are grave consequences to an idealized concept of "nature" as a pristine wilderness, separate from mankind, that people can only visit. Such a concept leaves our immediate surroundings unrecognized, unvalued, and unprotected. In this way, Smith's photographs of the Trinity are similar to the work of contemporary photographers such as Frank Gohlke, who recently completed a project on the Sudberry River in Massachusetts. The Sudberry, like the Trinity, is important because it is ordinary and typical, not spectacular and unusual. "Where we live has a far greater effect on the real quality of our lives than what we visit," Gohlke wrote.

Smith shares a great deal with other contemporary photographers in both his ecological outlook and his contemplative and subtle style. His understated style is clearly allied to that of the generation of photographers first recognized in the 1974 seminal New Topographic exhibition at the George Eastman House. Like Robert Adams, Frank Gohlke, and Nicholas Nixon among others featured in that show, Smith does not impose artificial drama on a scene or follow Ansel Adams' pursuit of unusual vantage points or fleeting moments of dramatic lighting that present the landscape in a heightened mode that few of us get to experience. Smith is also in accord with many of his contemporaries who have developed a passionate commitment to ecological issues and the need to preserve, value, and respect seemingly conventional landscapes that we have come to take for granted. Perhaps the greatest strength is that Smith has arrived at these positions naturally on his own, not because they are trendy.

If his photographs of teenage rodeo marked Smith's struggles with the party days of youth and the awkward anxiety that comes with them, then his complex photographs of the river are the creation of a more mature individual who, like the river, has come to peace with himself. This introspective, contemplative quality may be the greatest reward of this series.

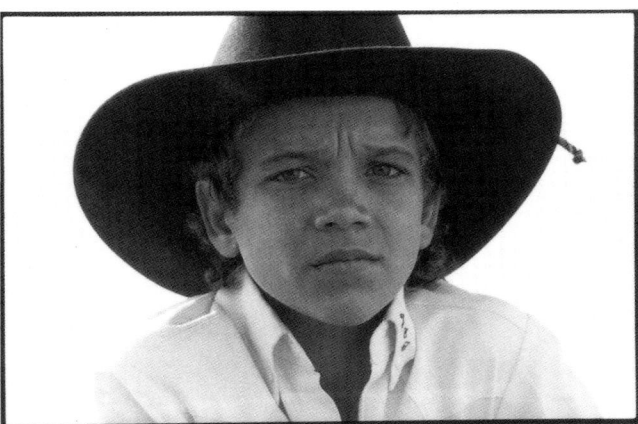

THE TRINITY RIVER

Photographs by Luther Smith

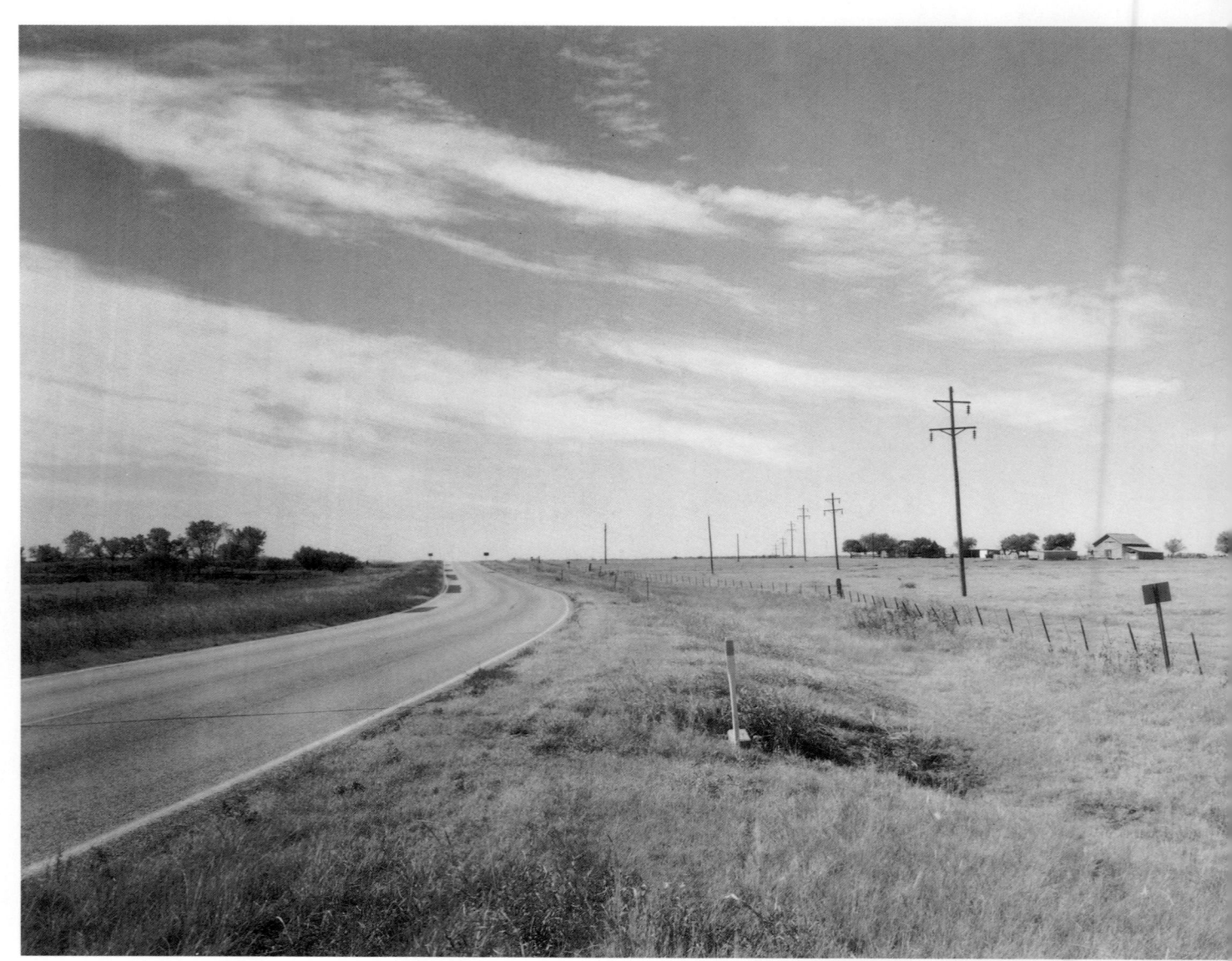

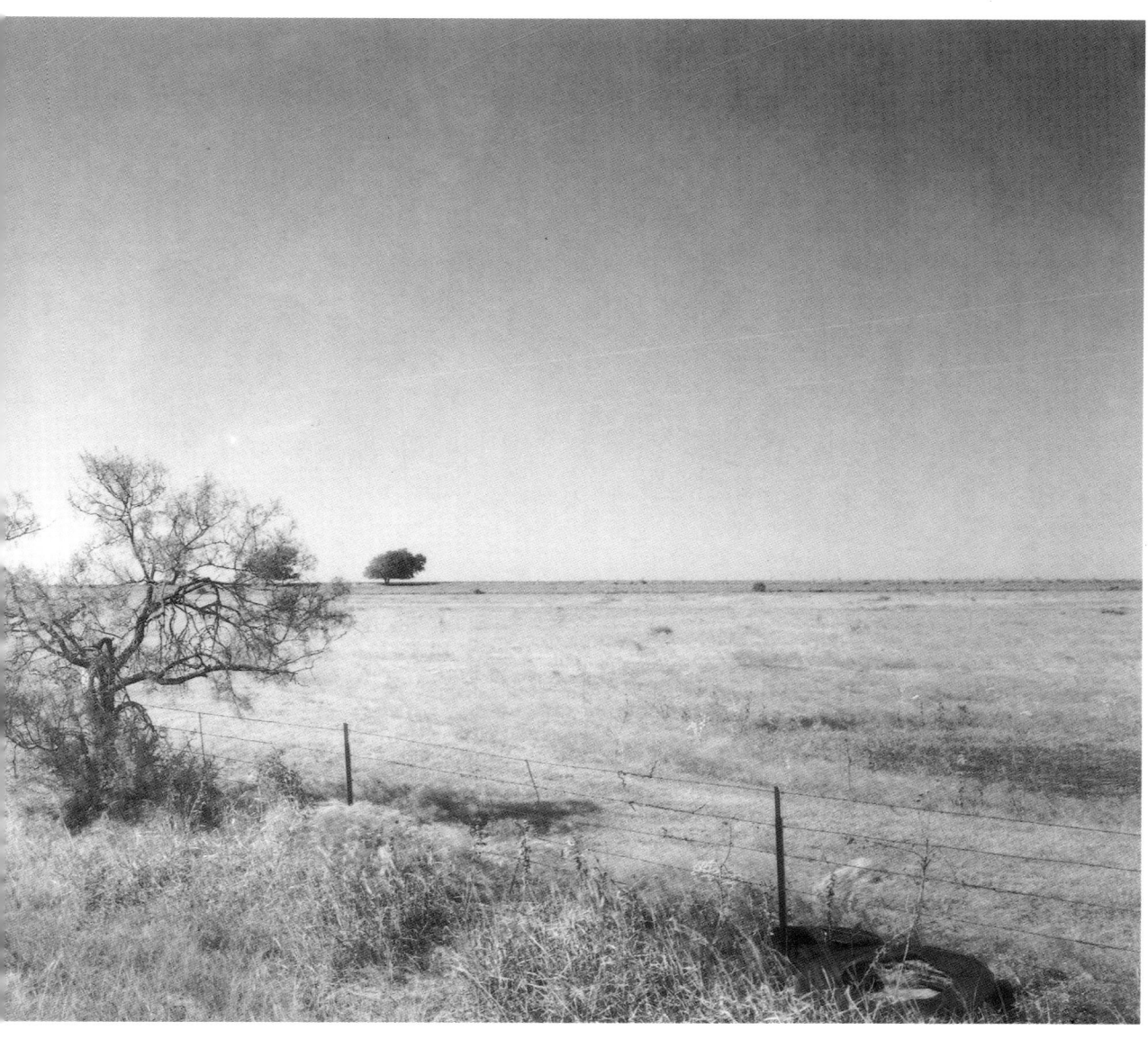

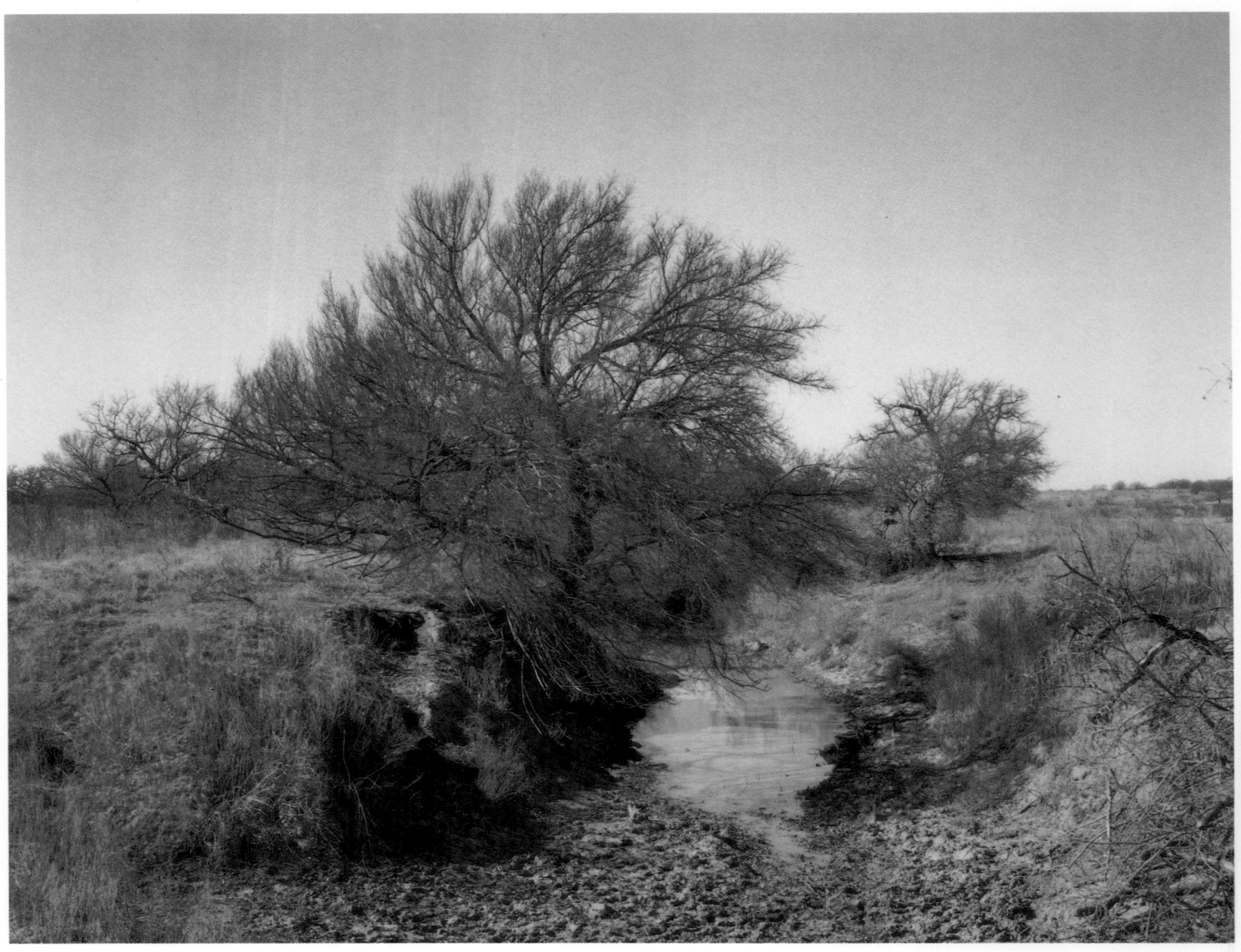

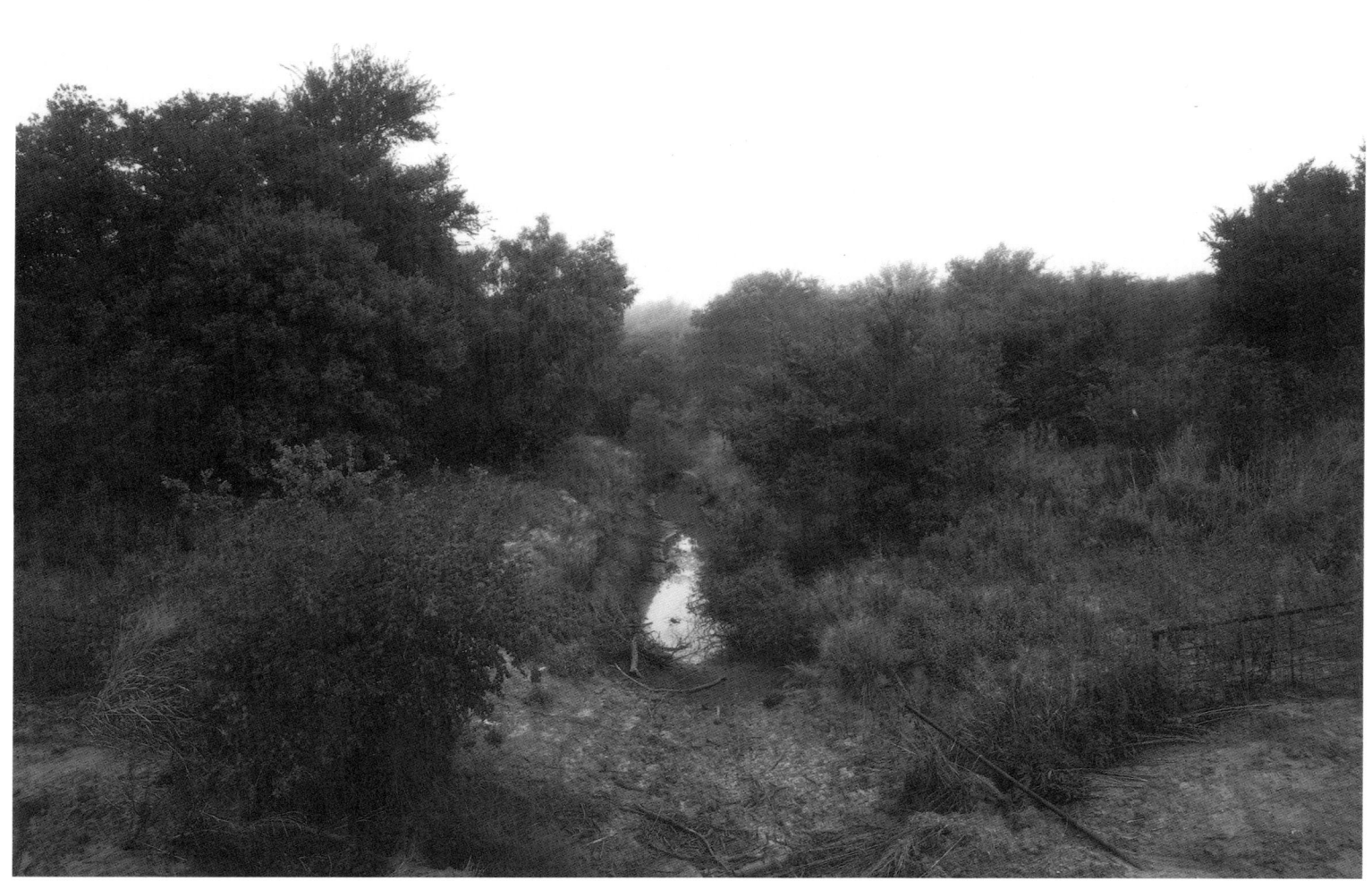

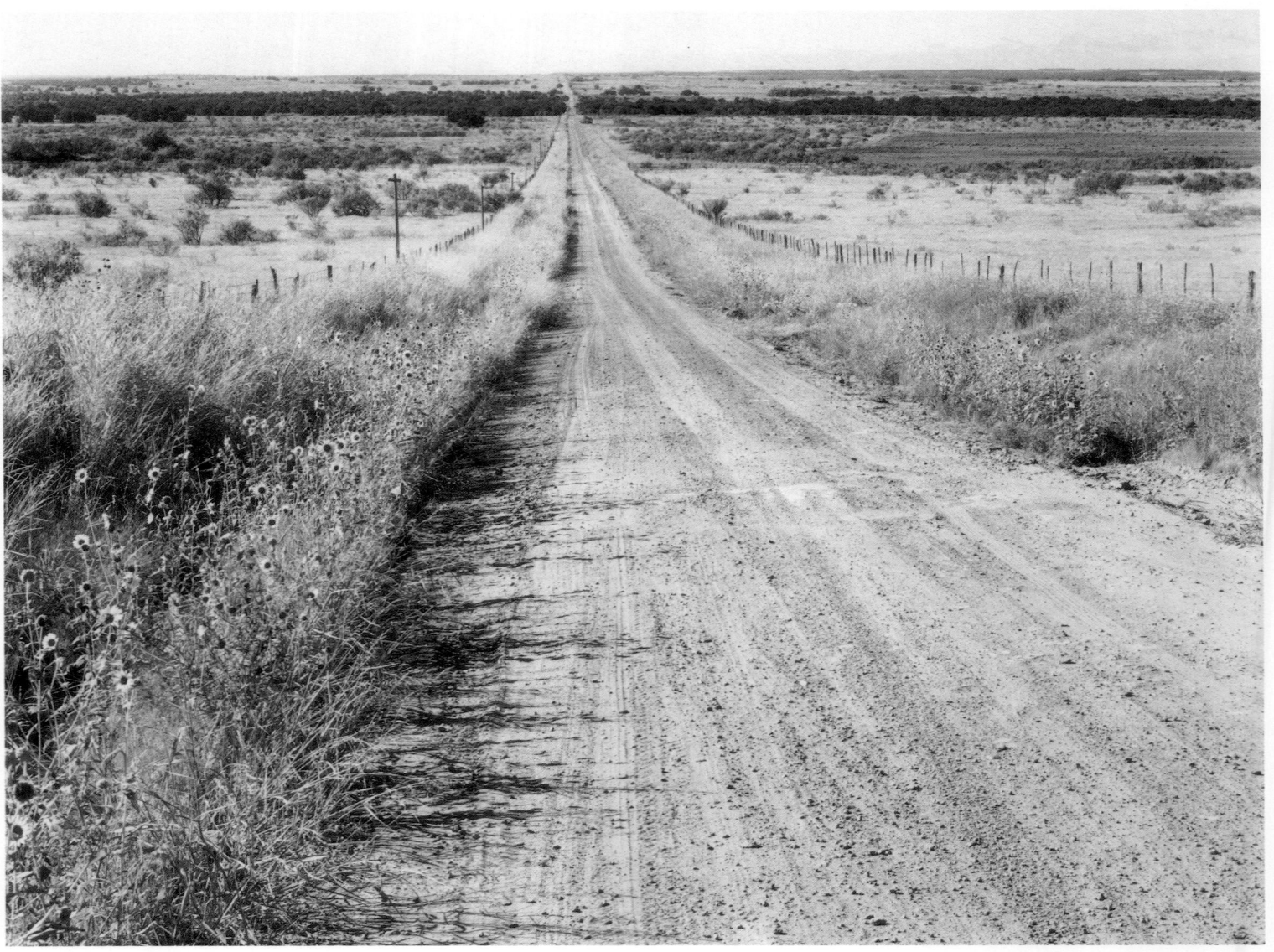

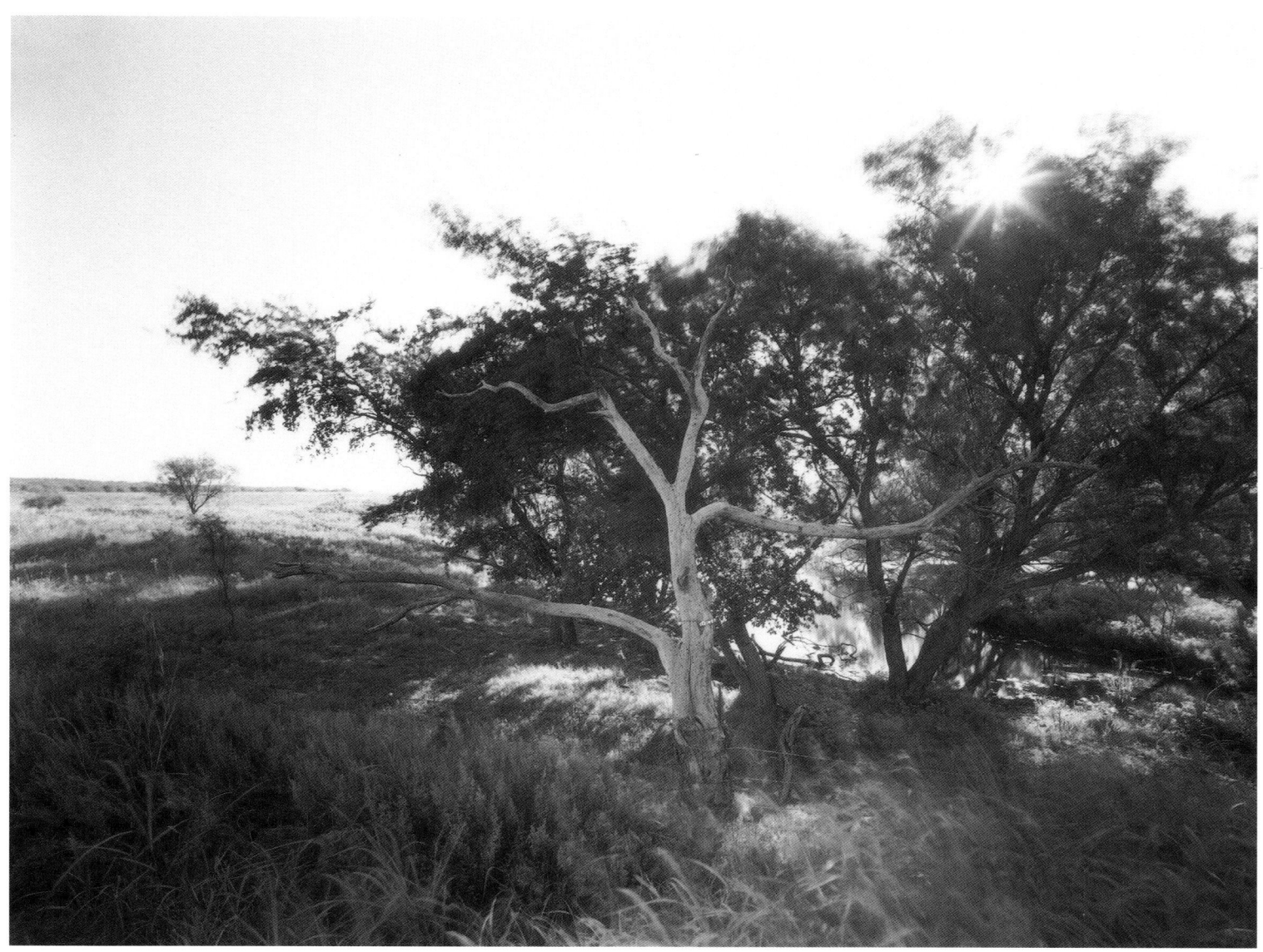

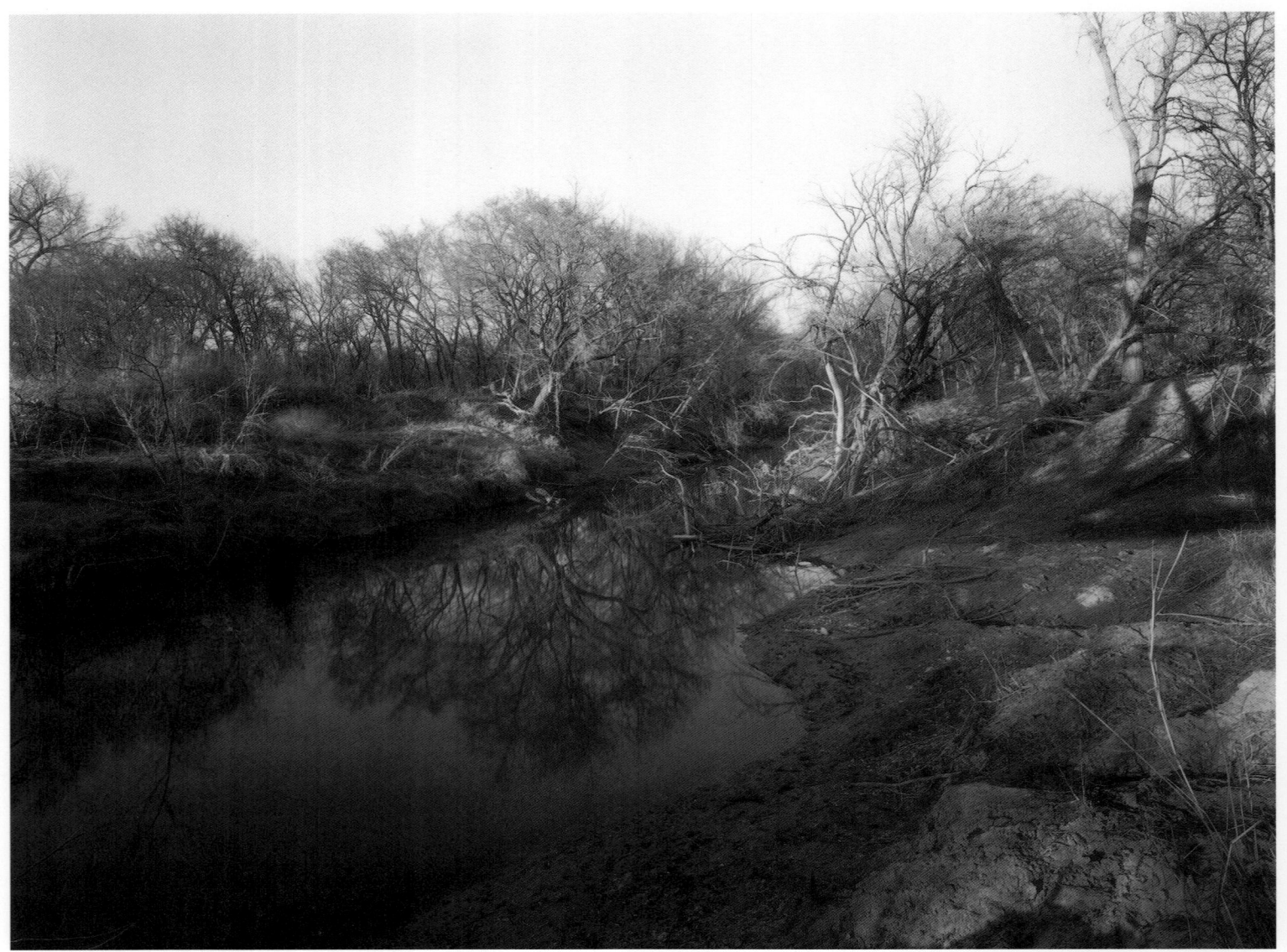

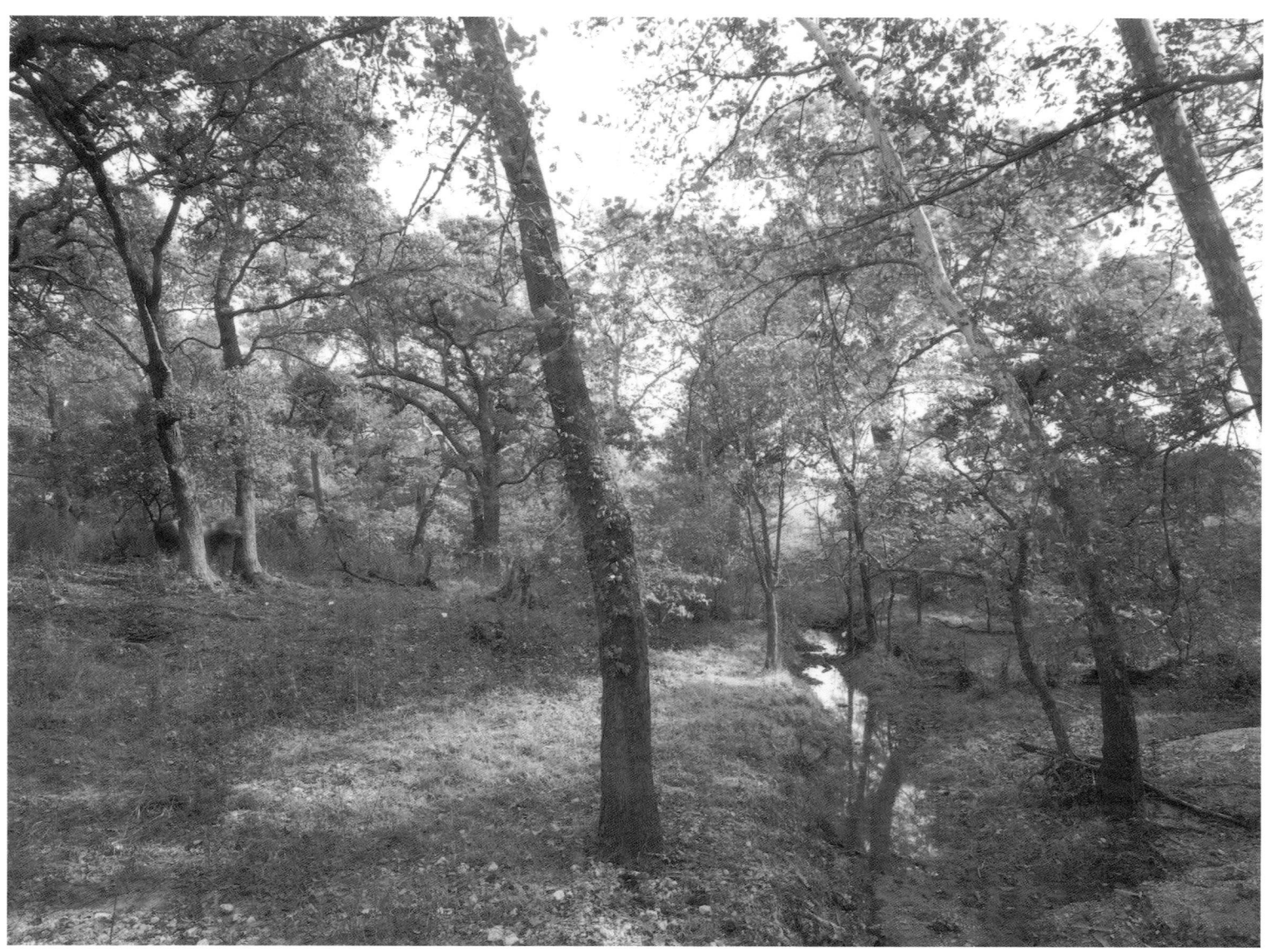

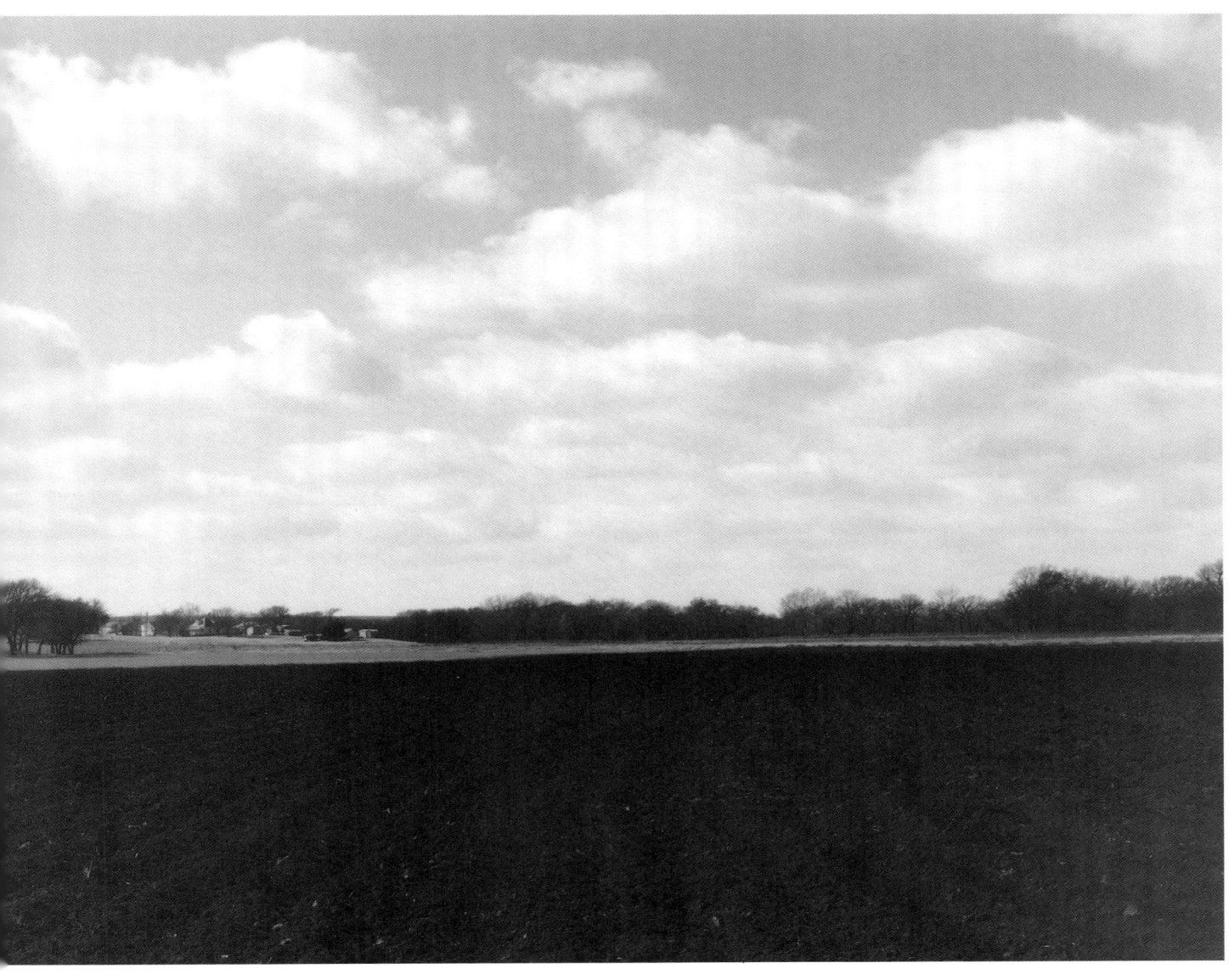

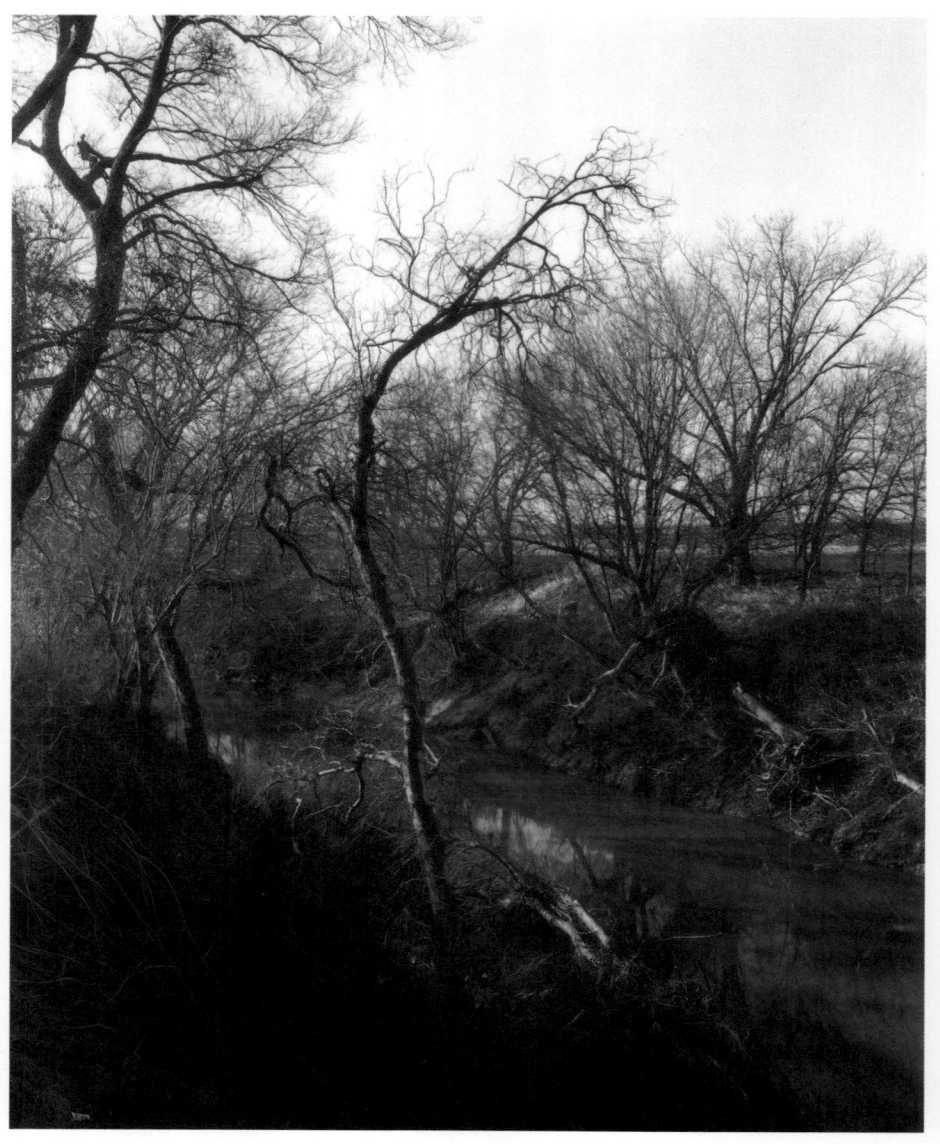

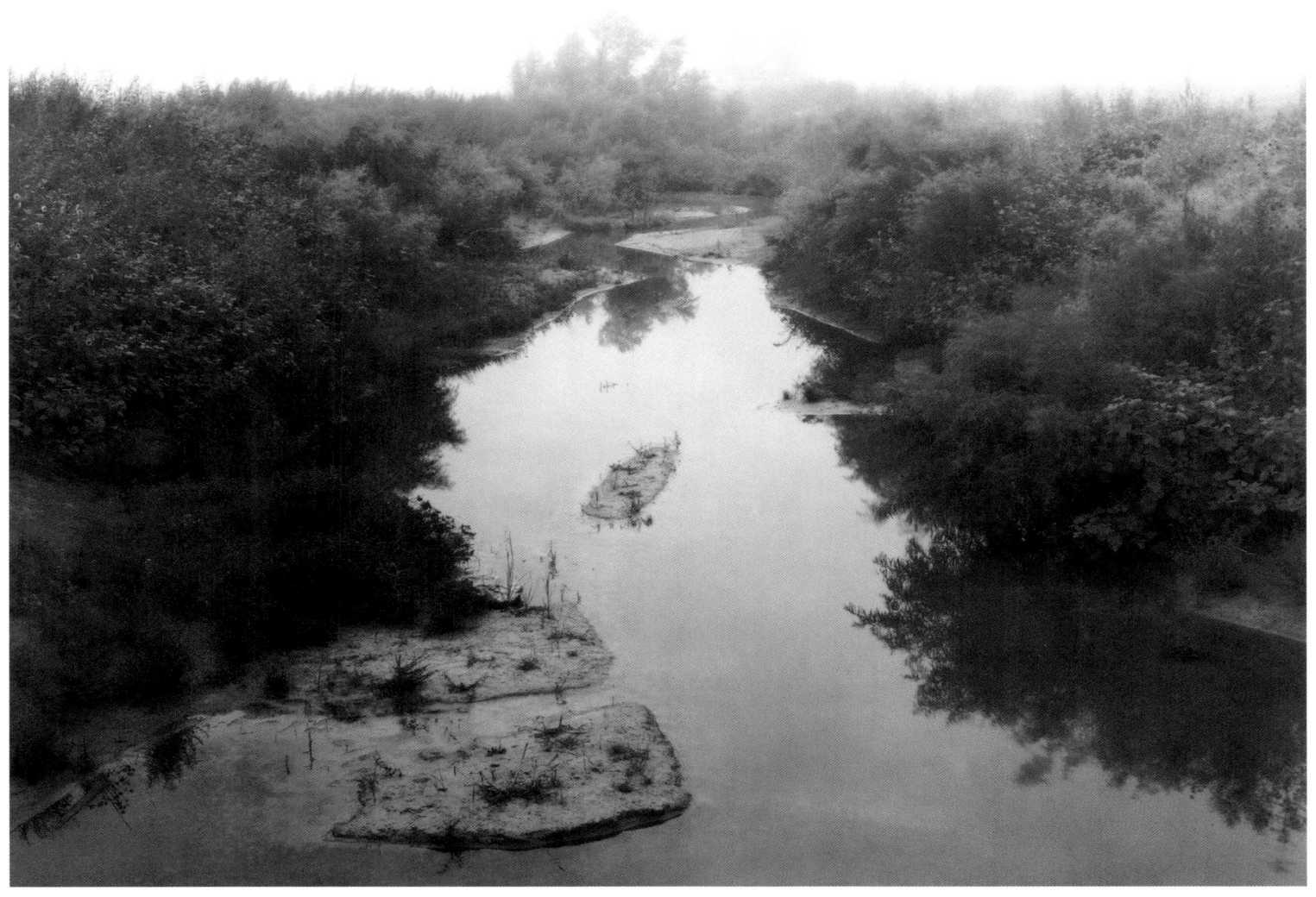

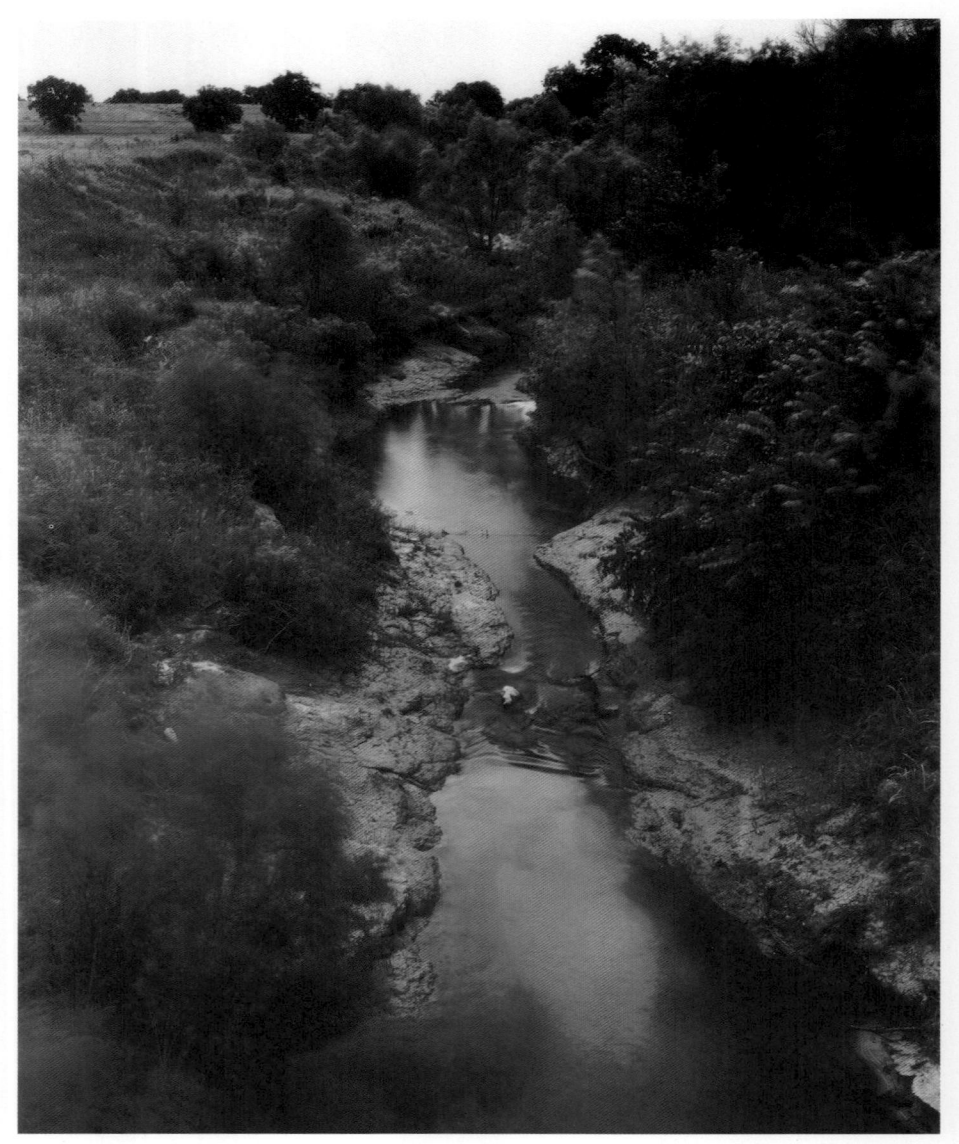

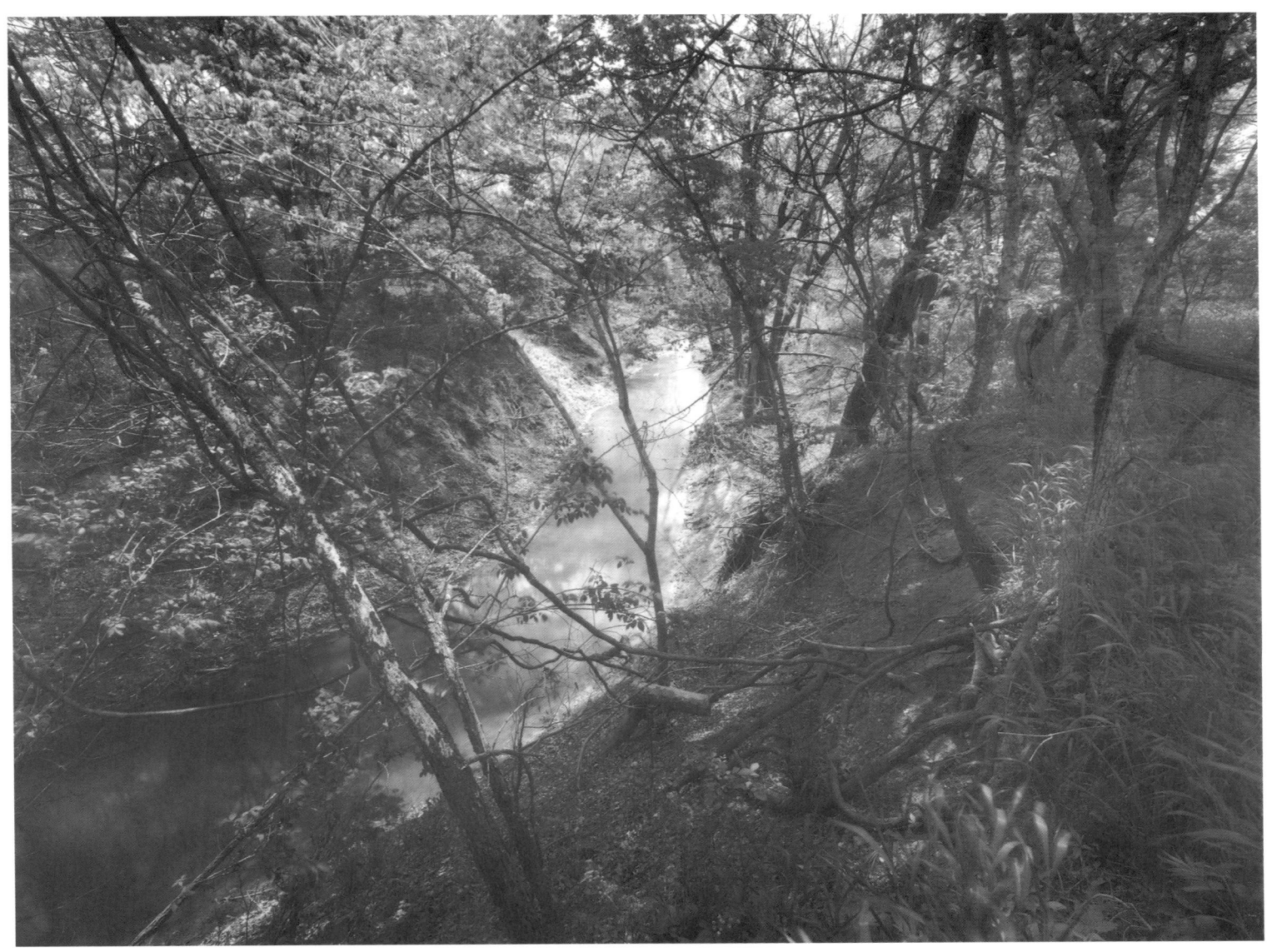

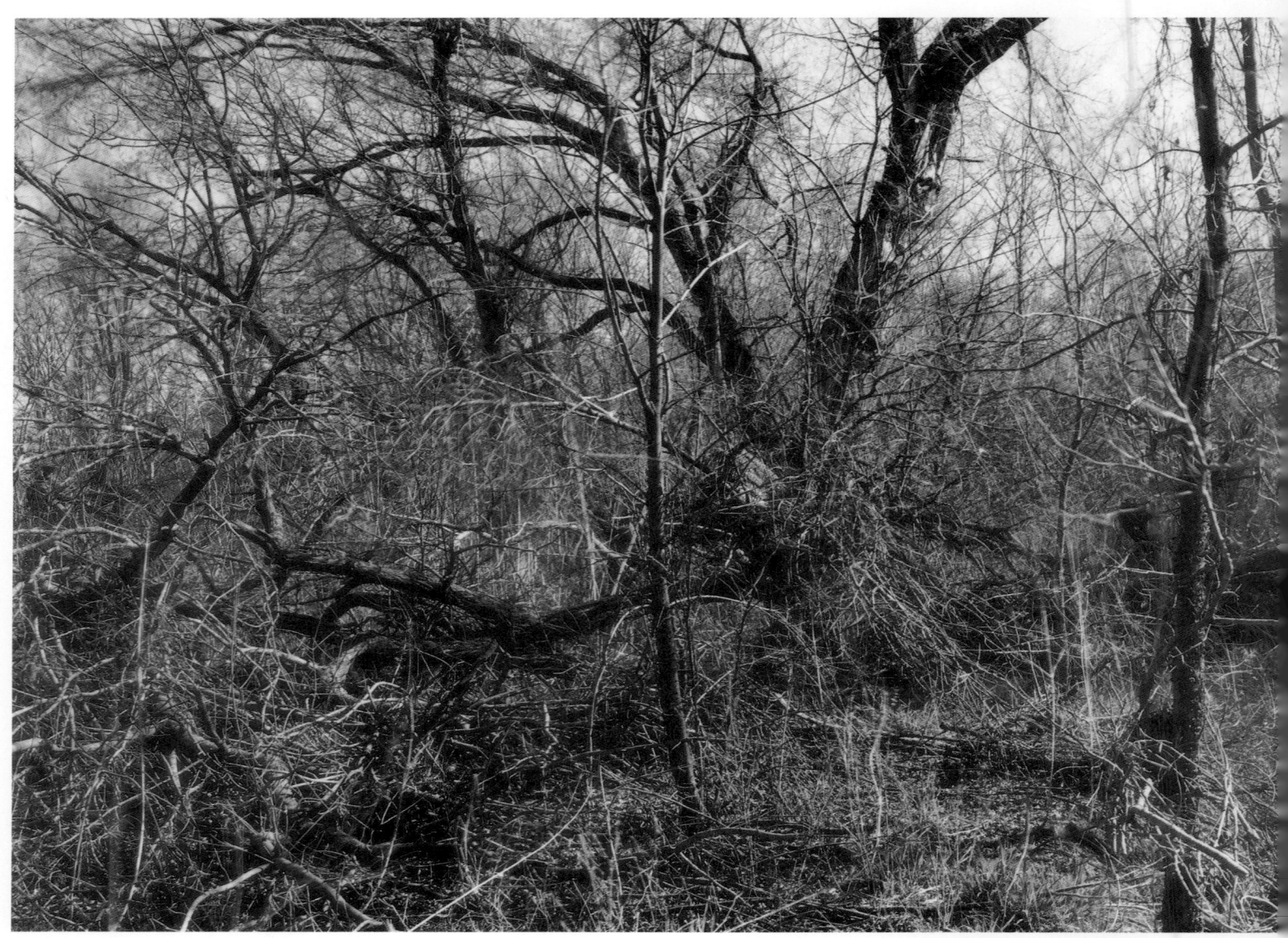

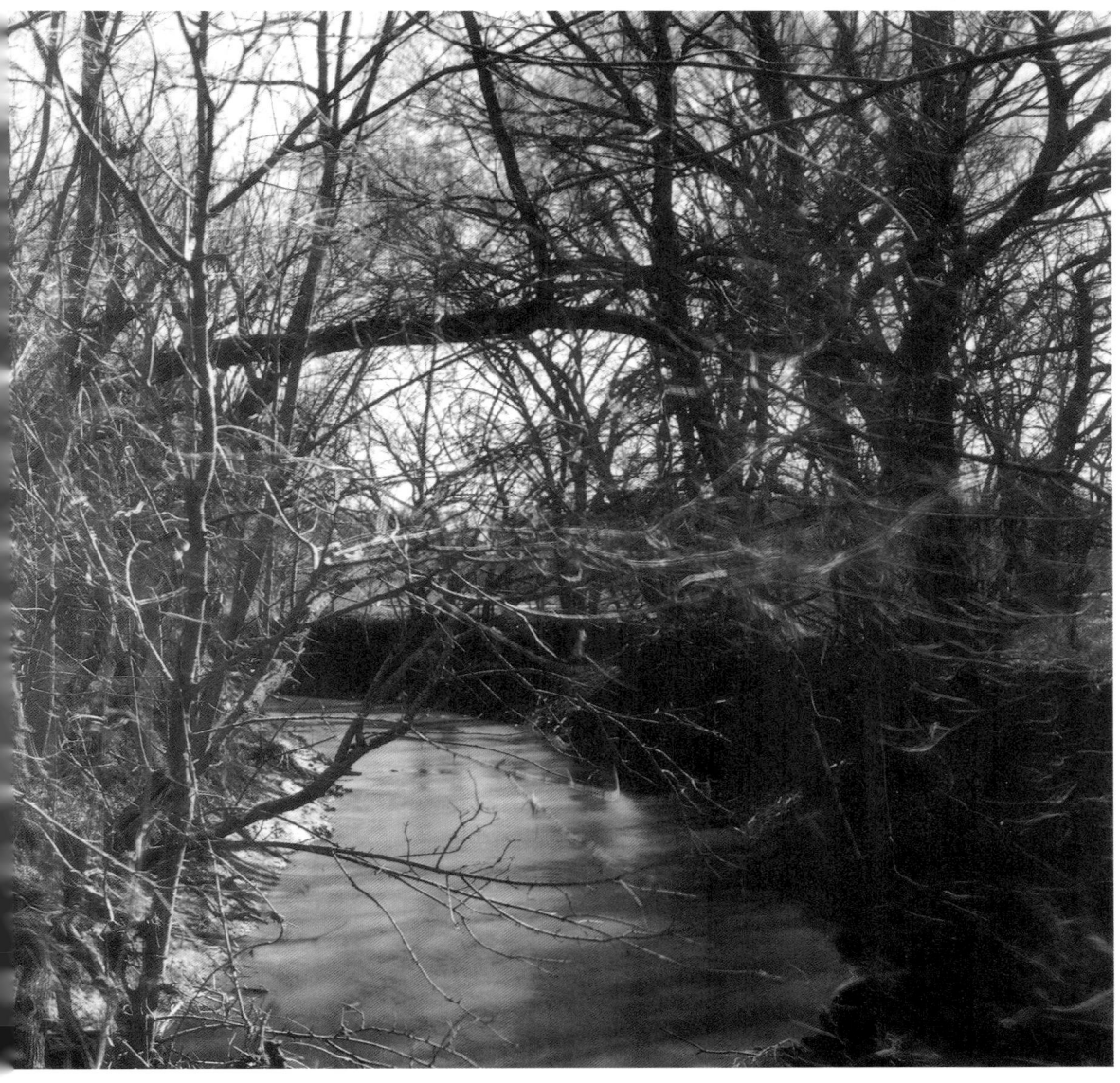

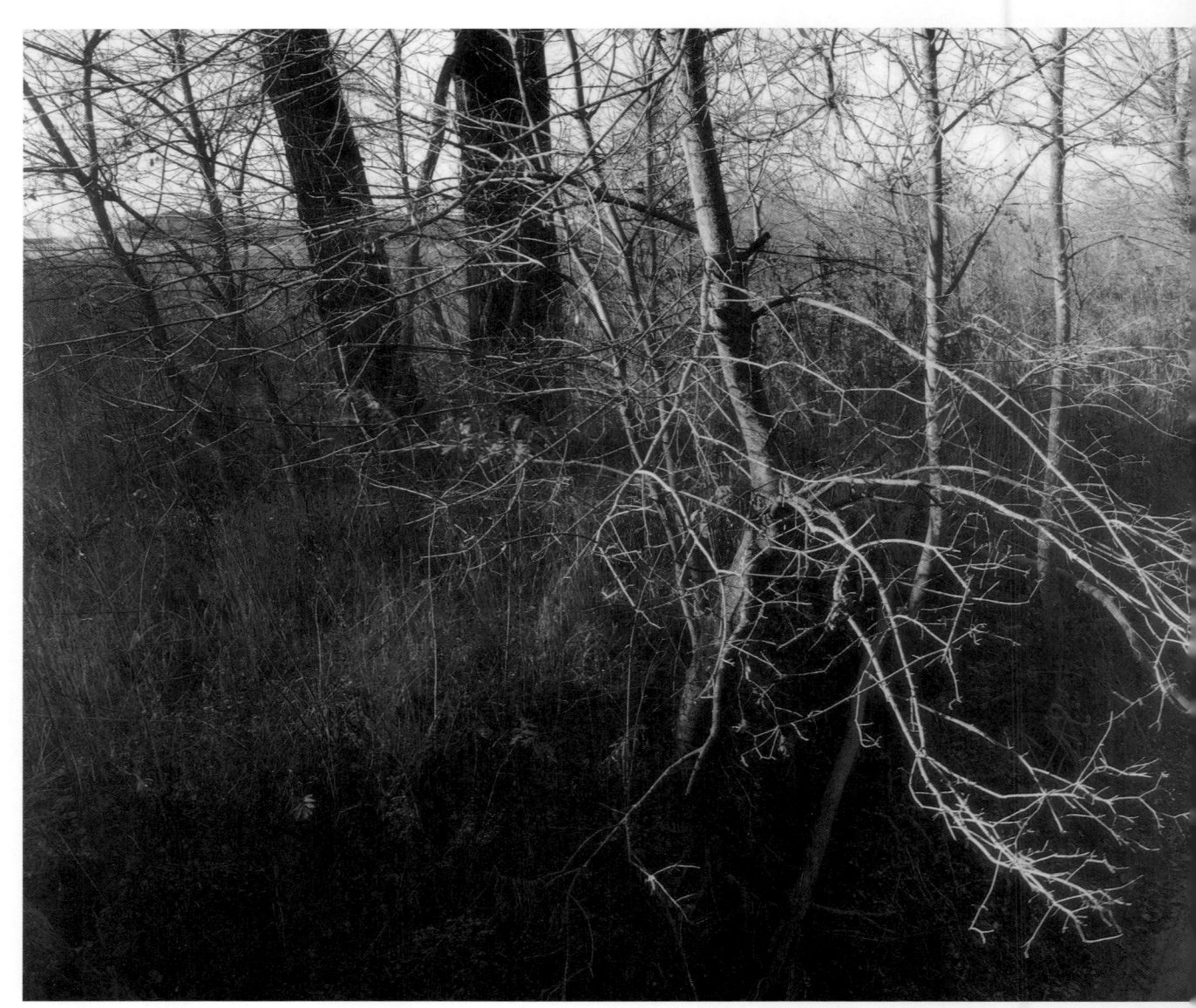

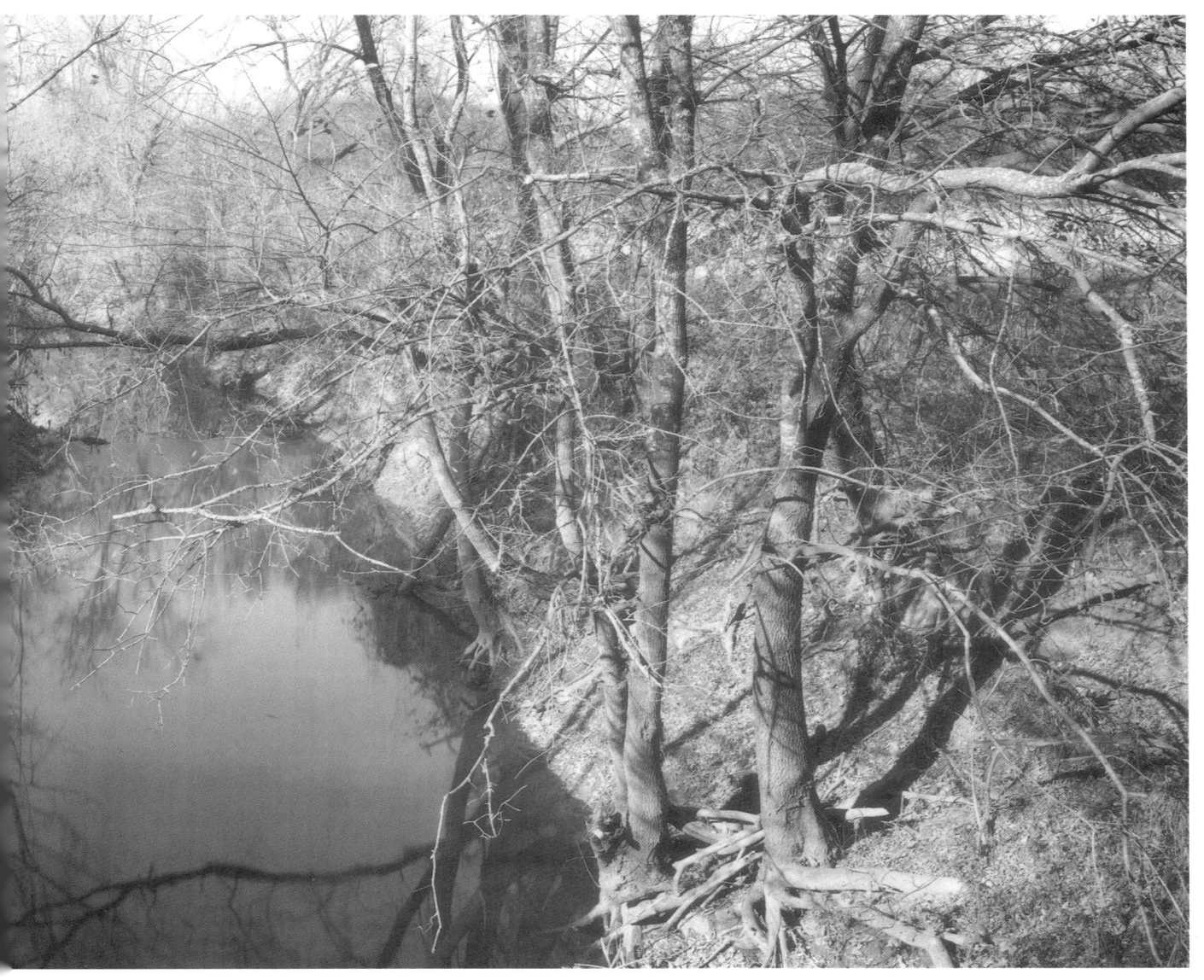

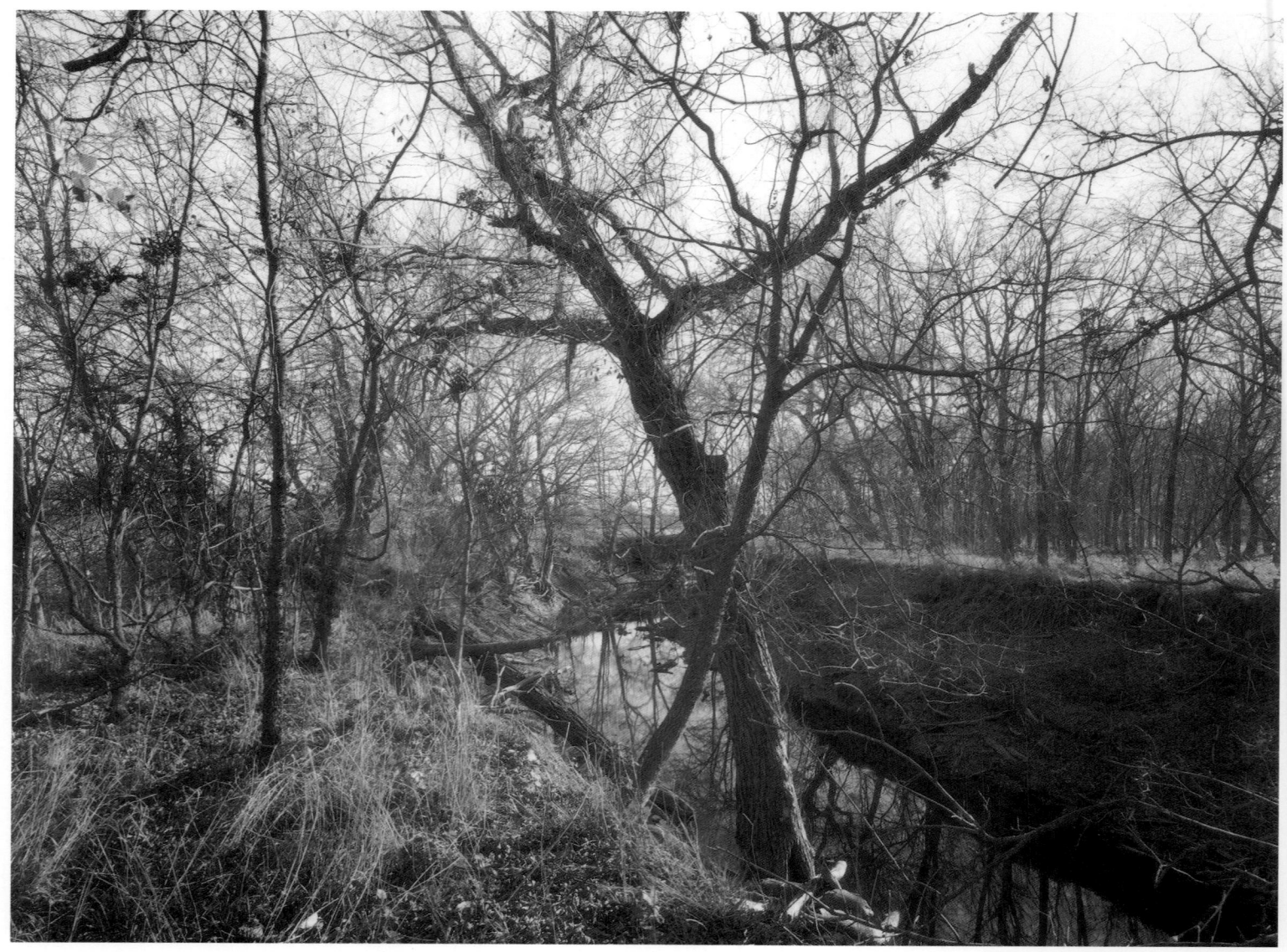

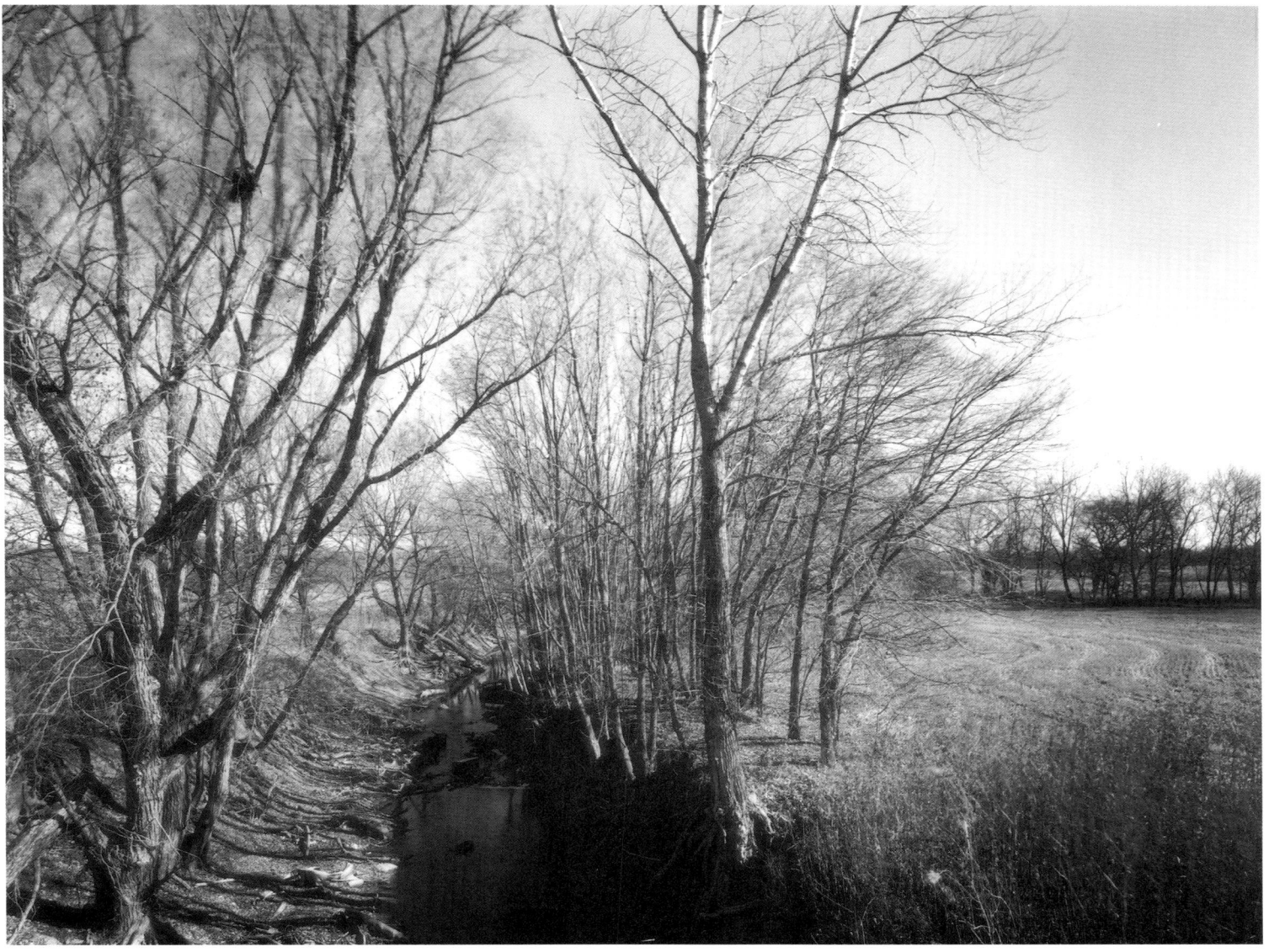

16

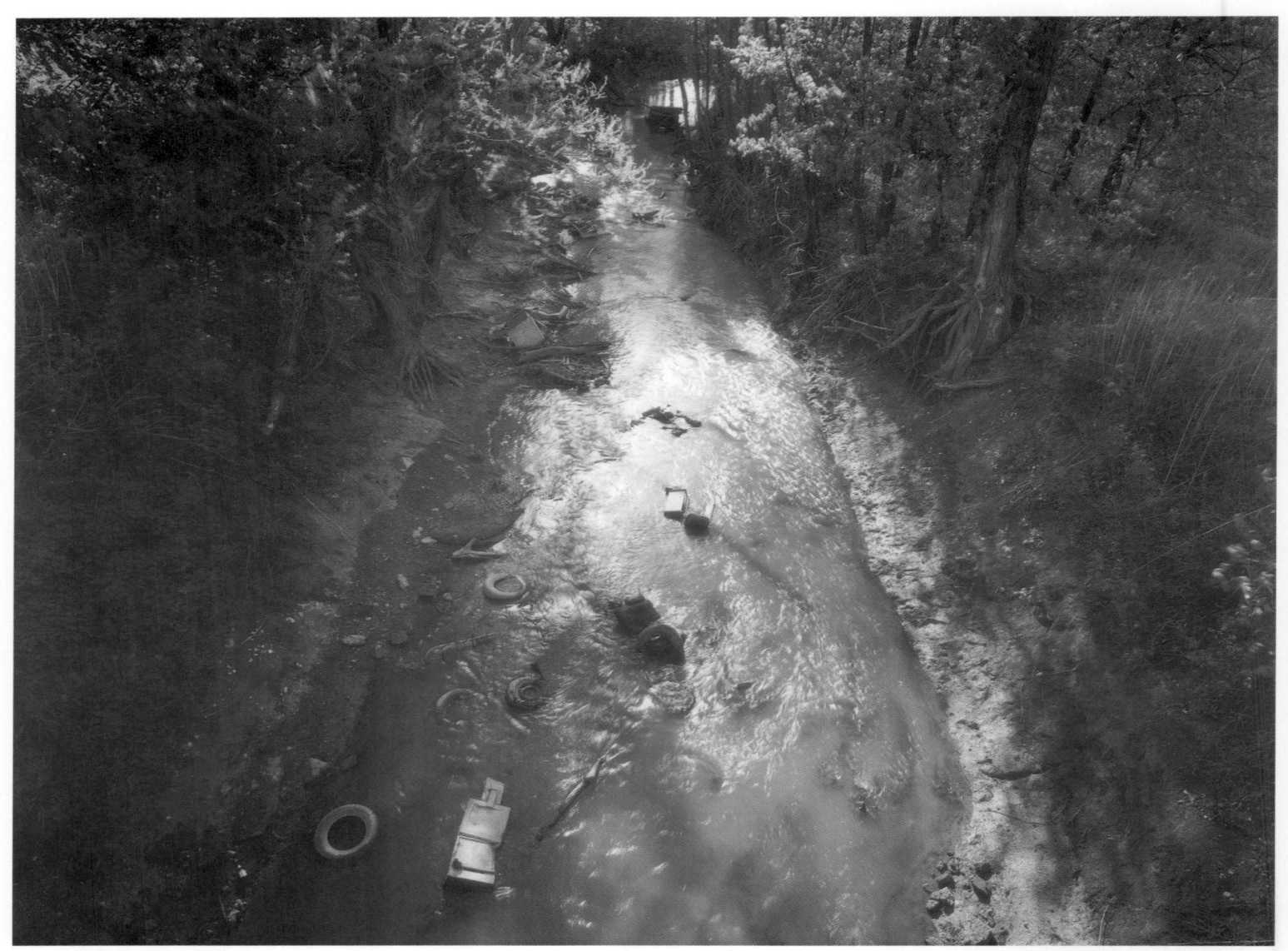

17

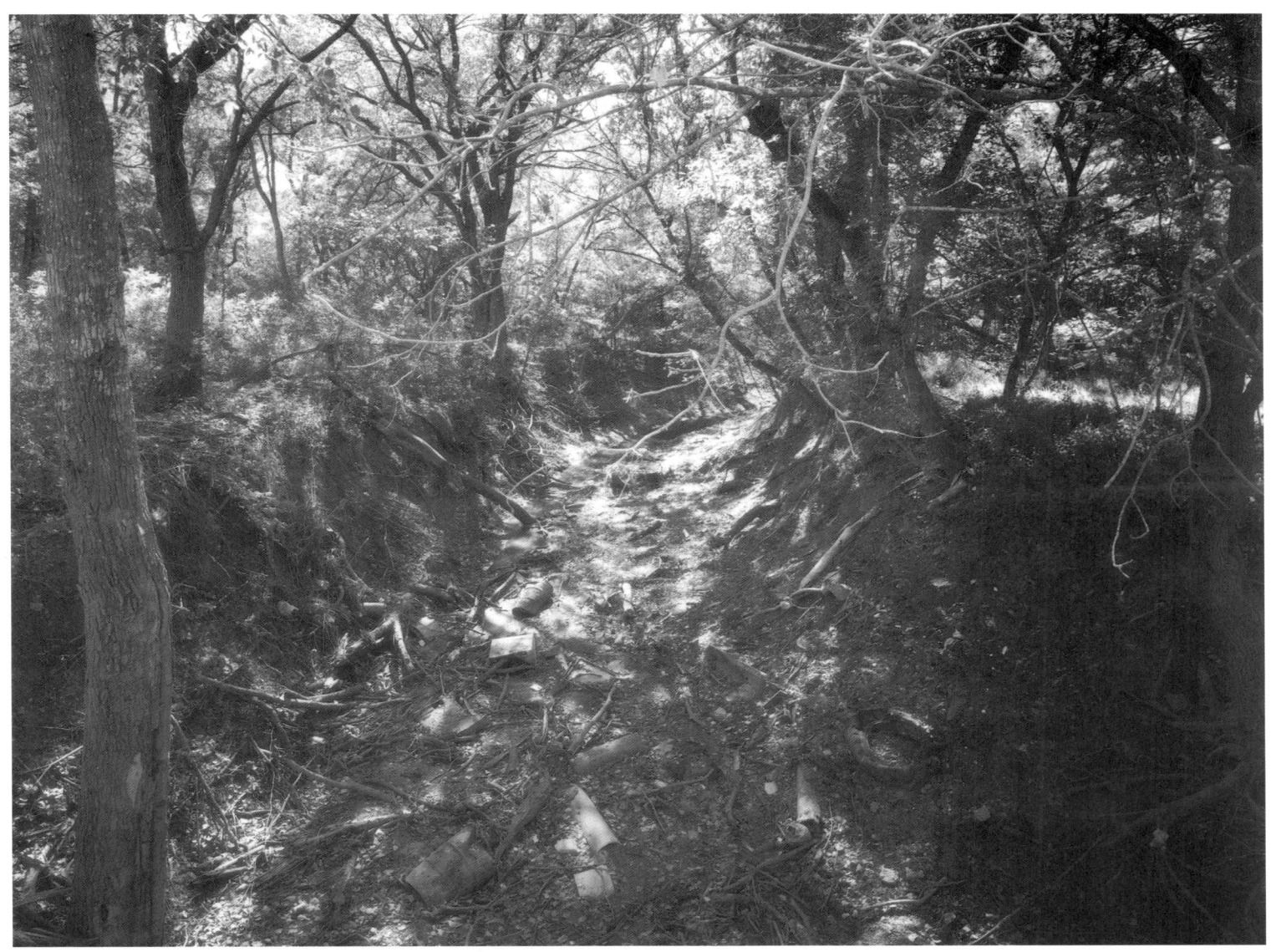

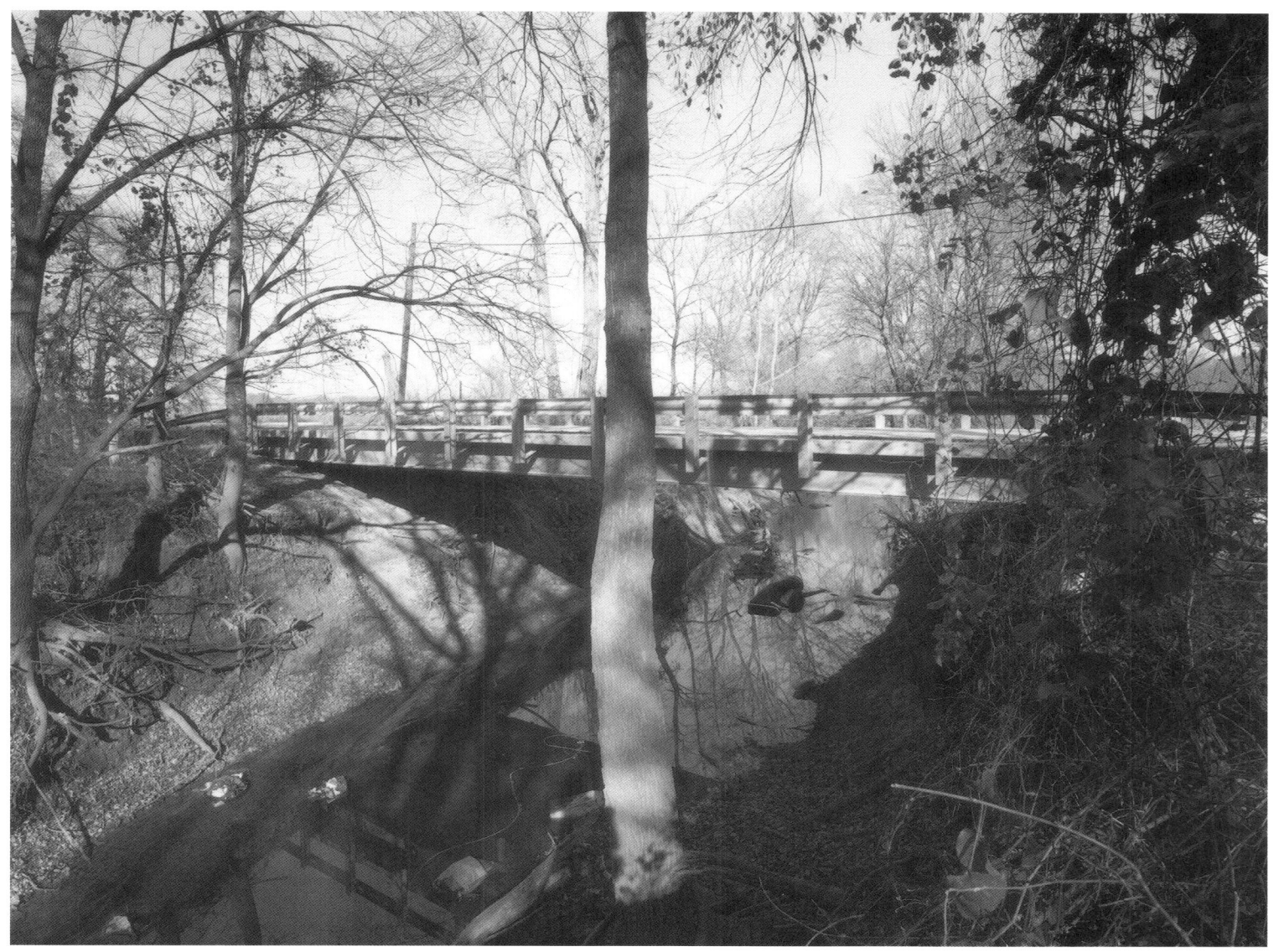

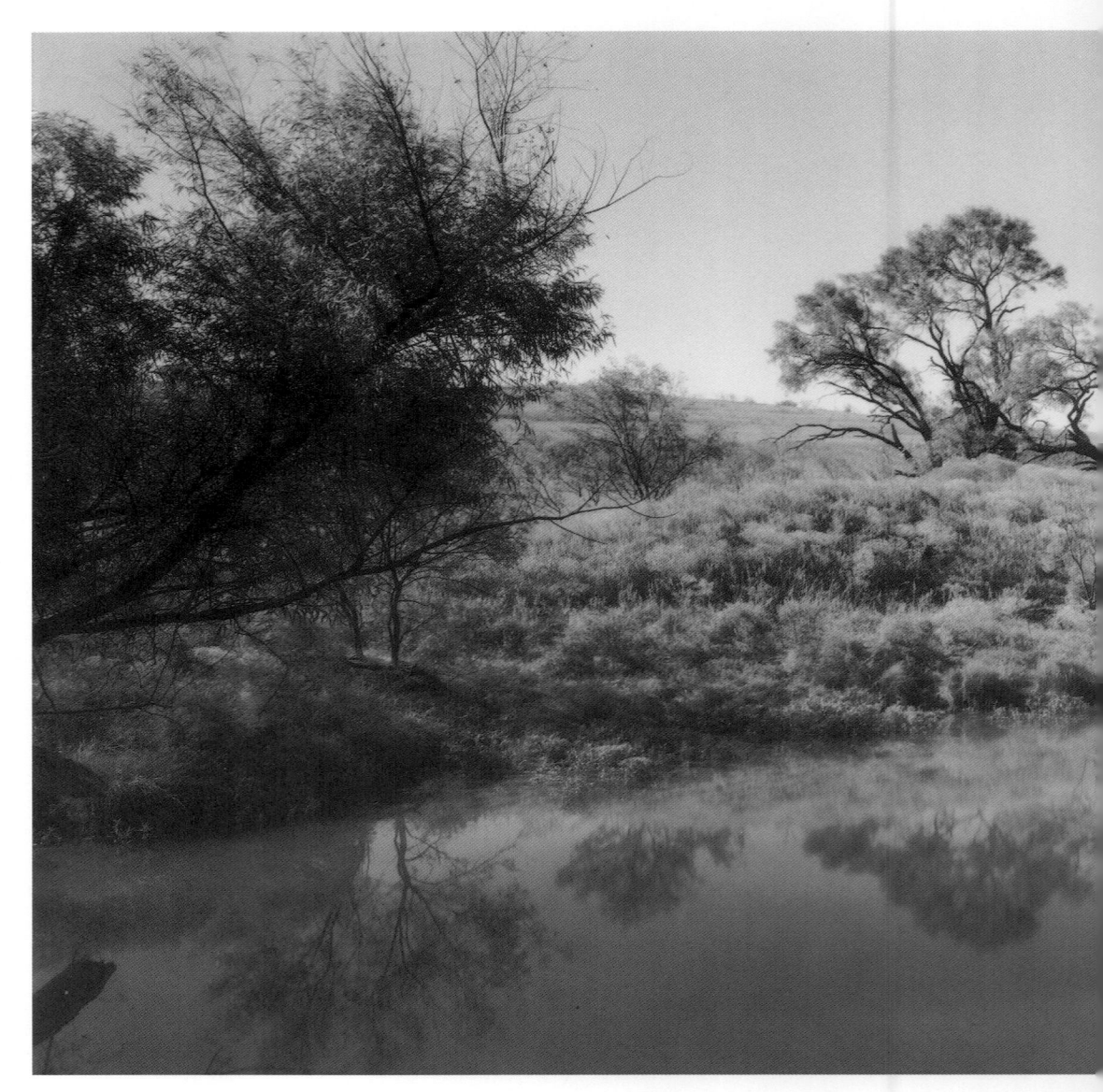

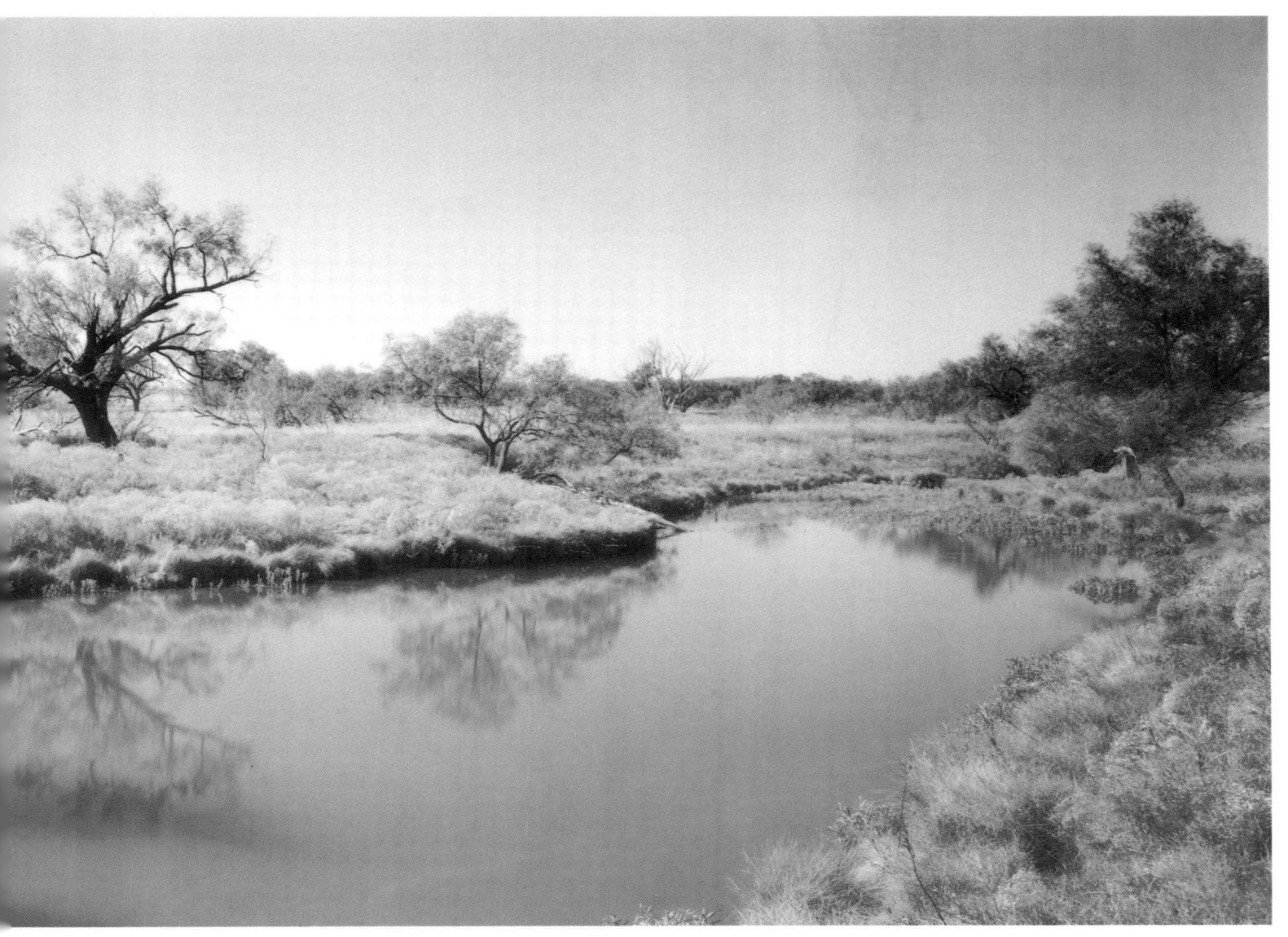

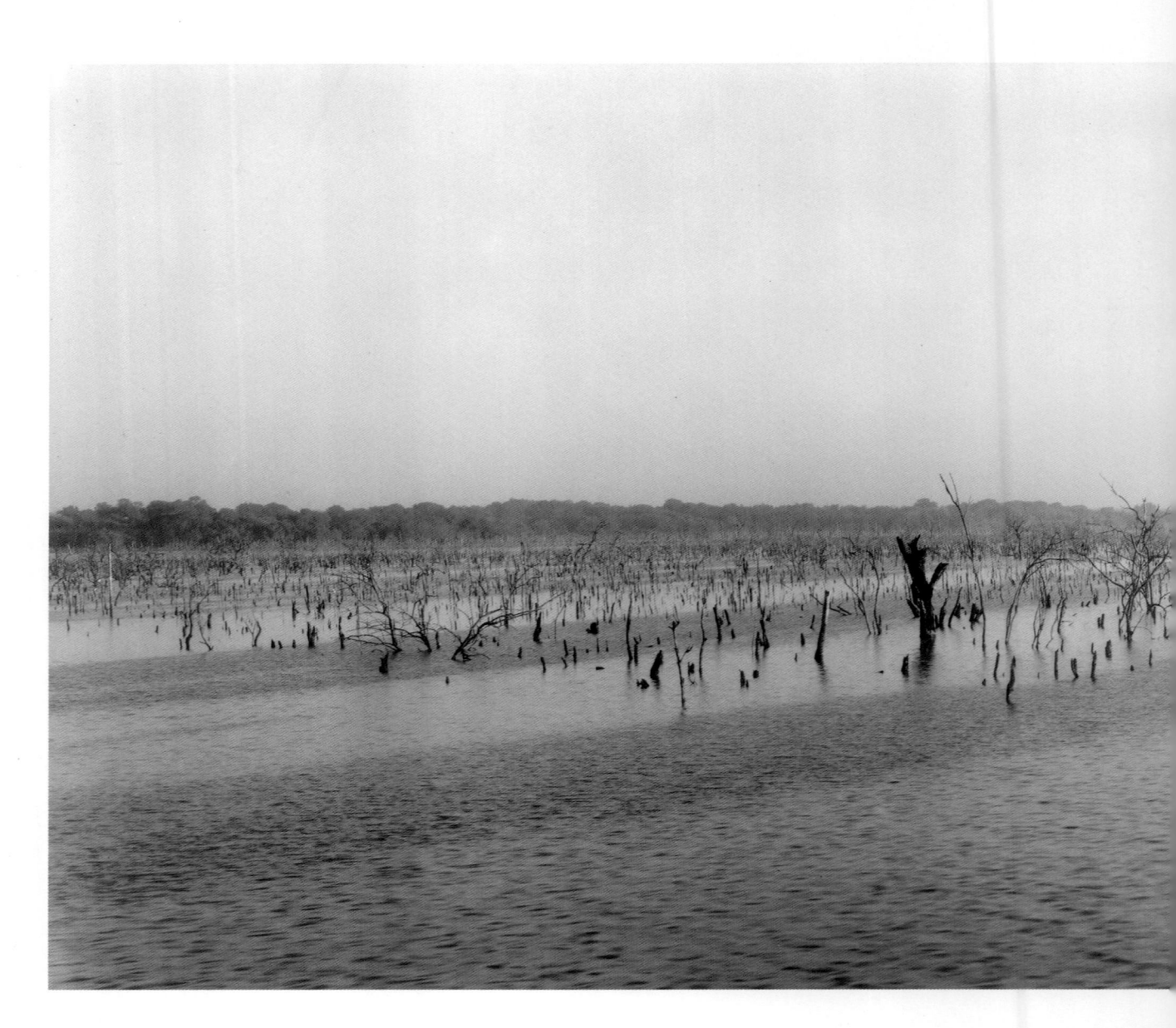

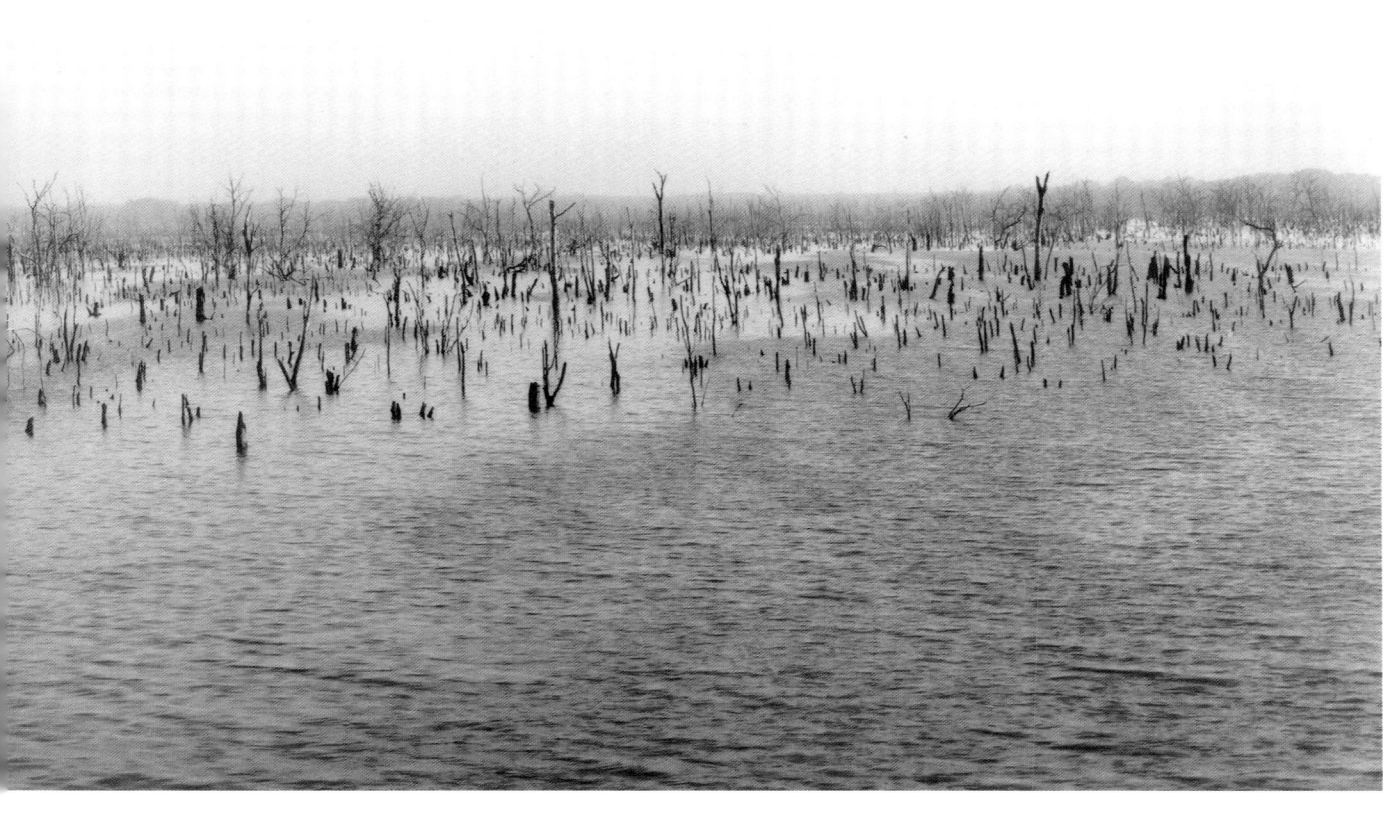

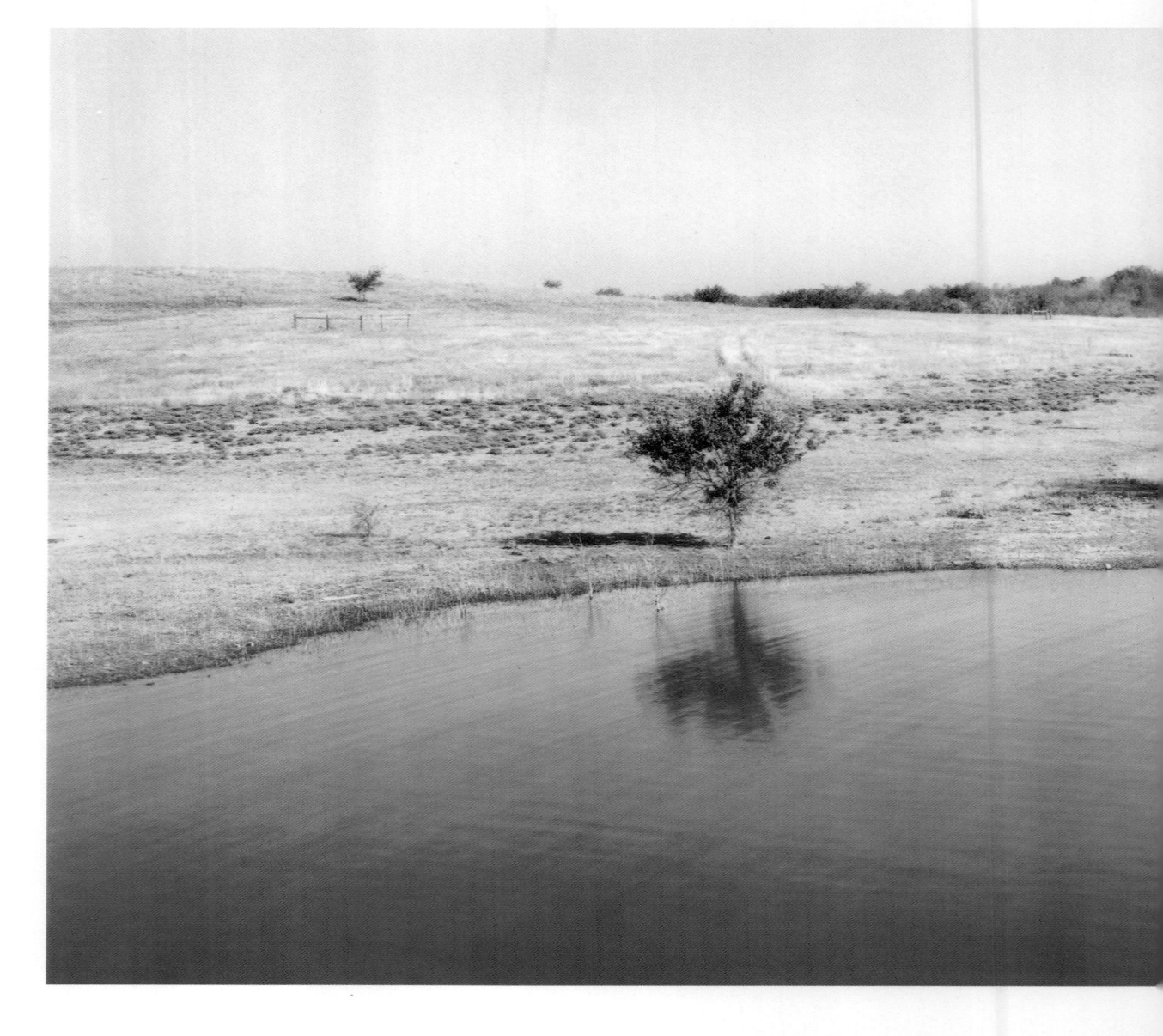

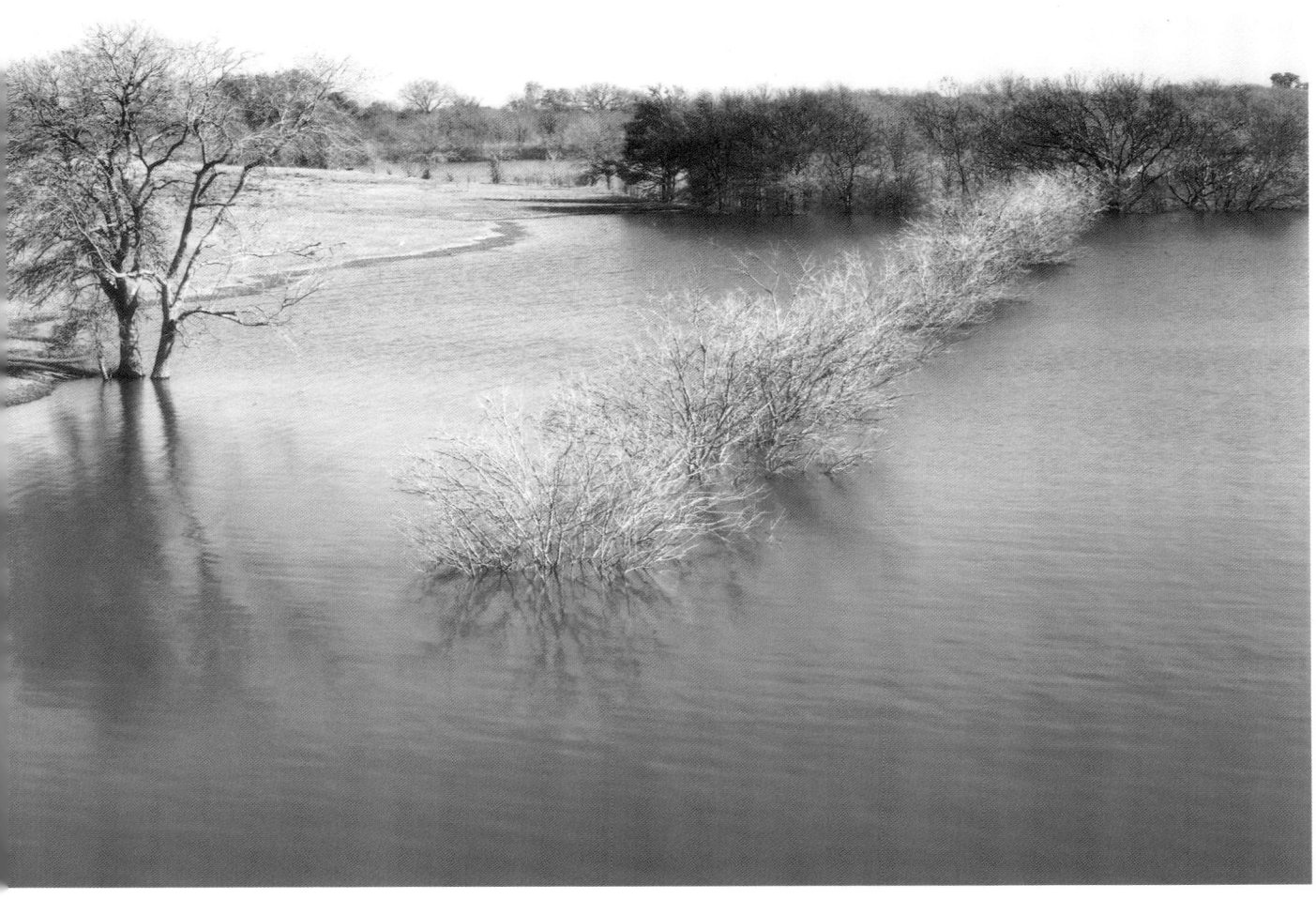

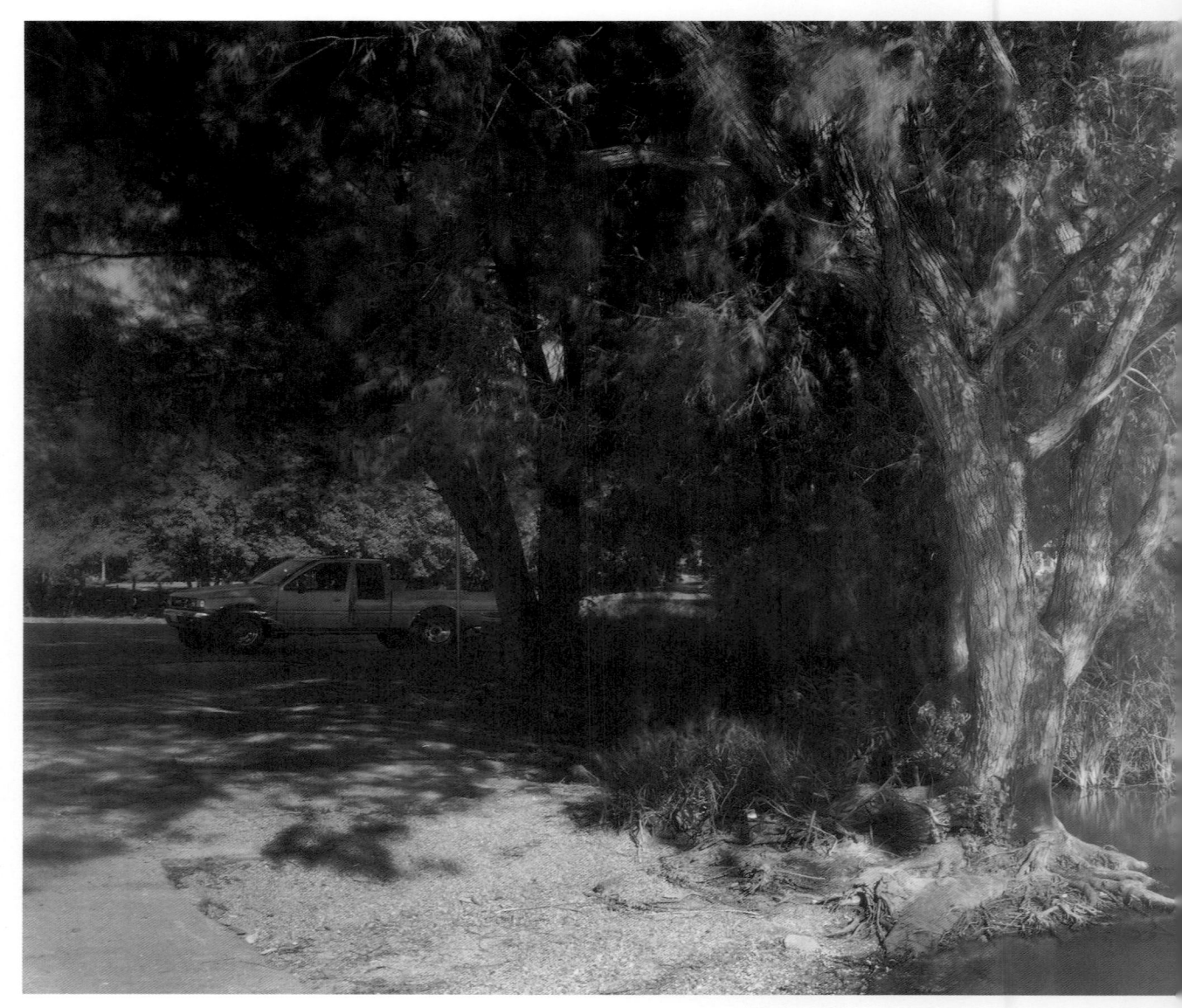

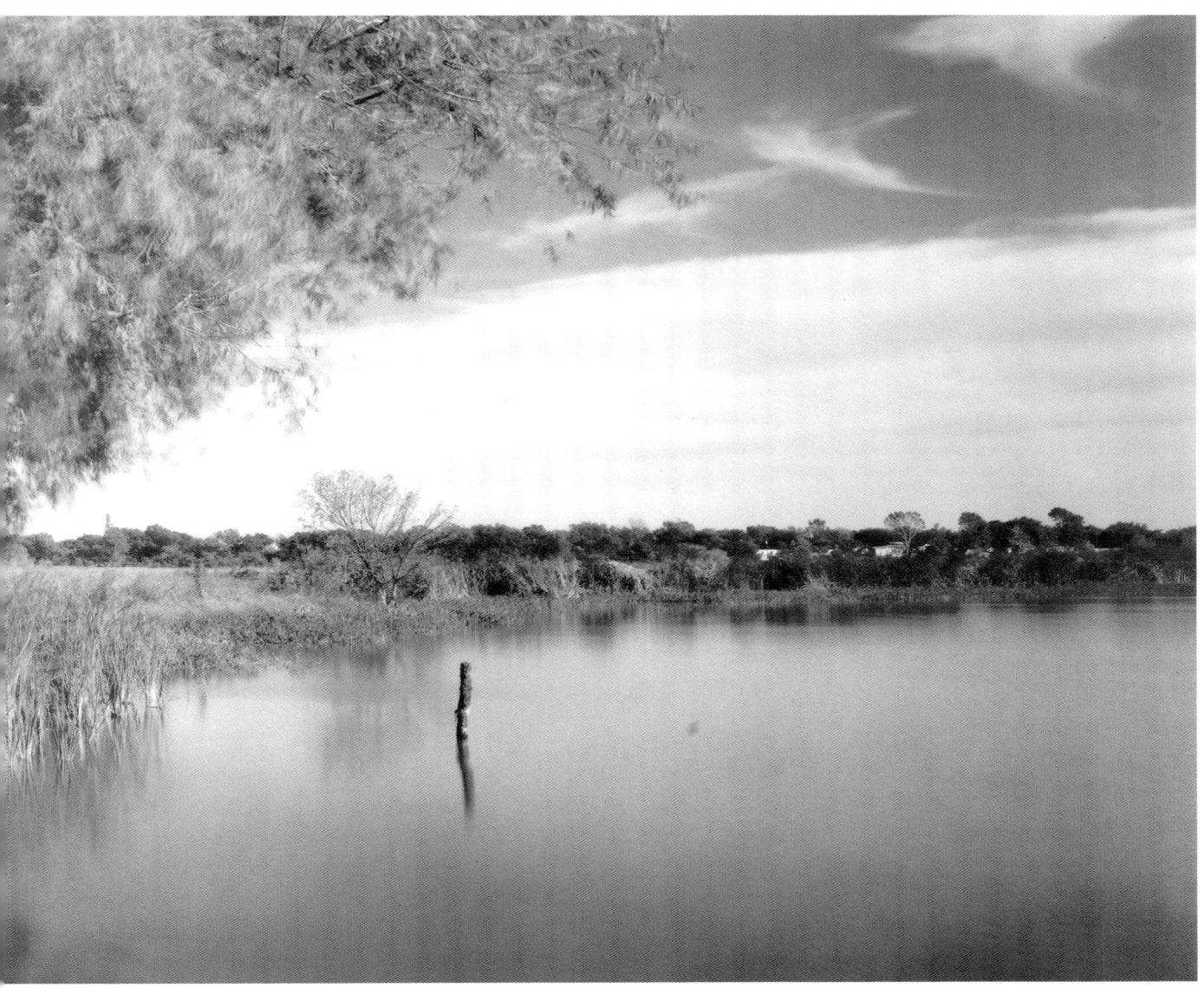

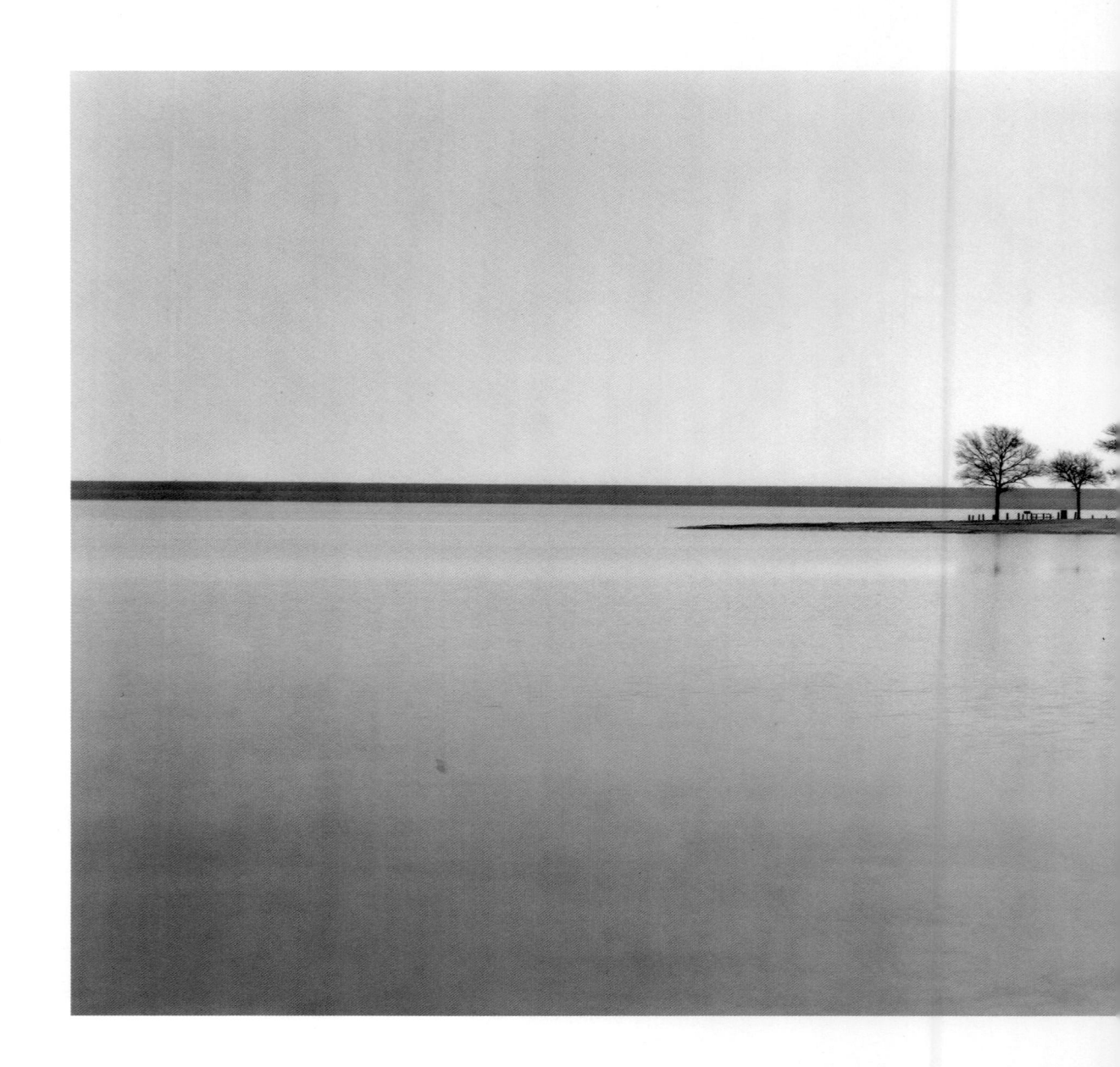

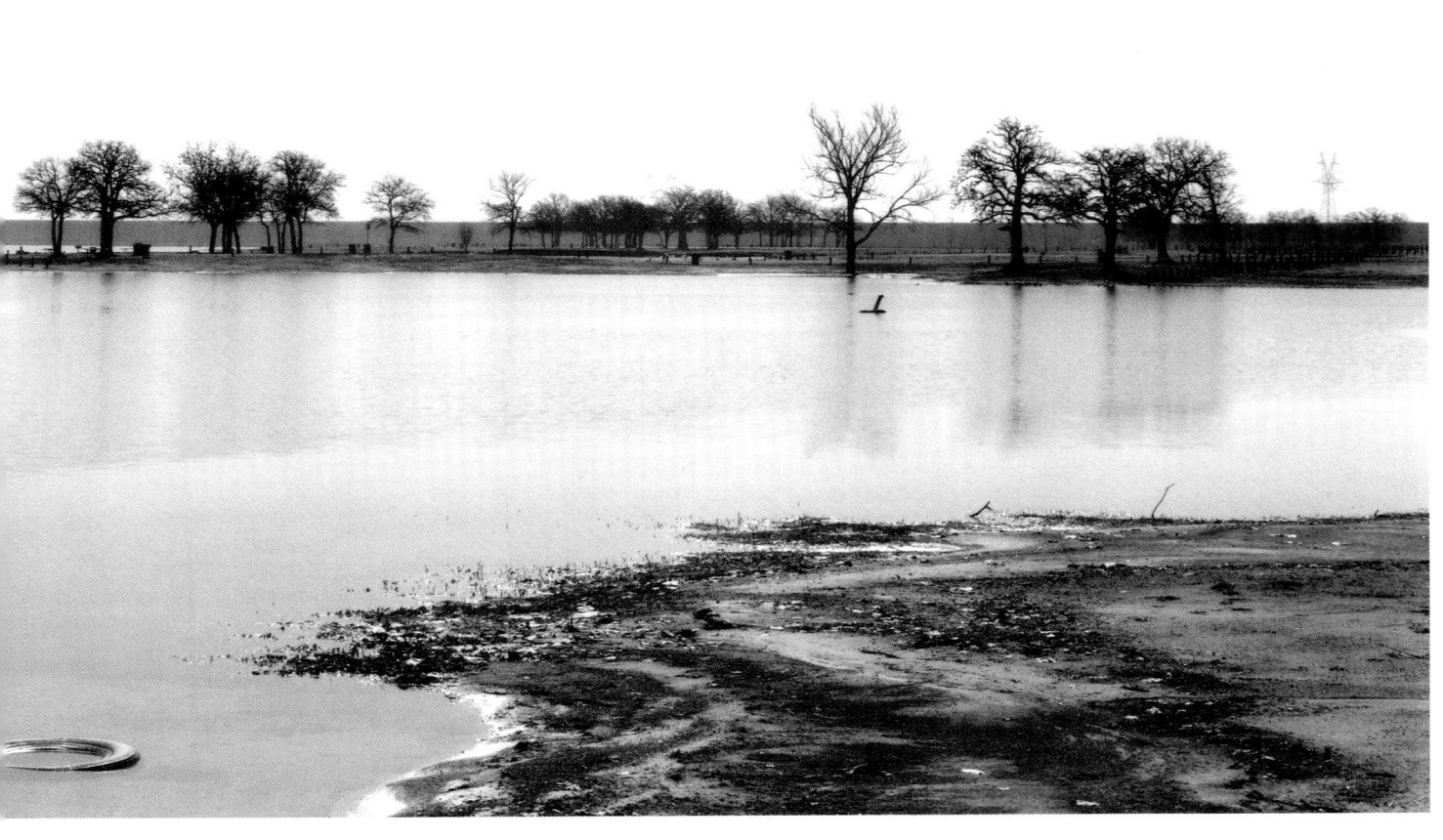

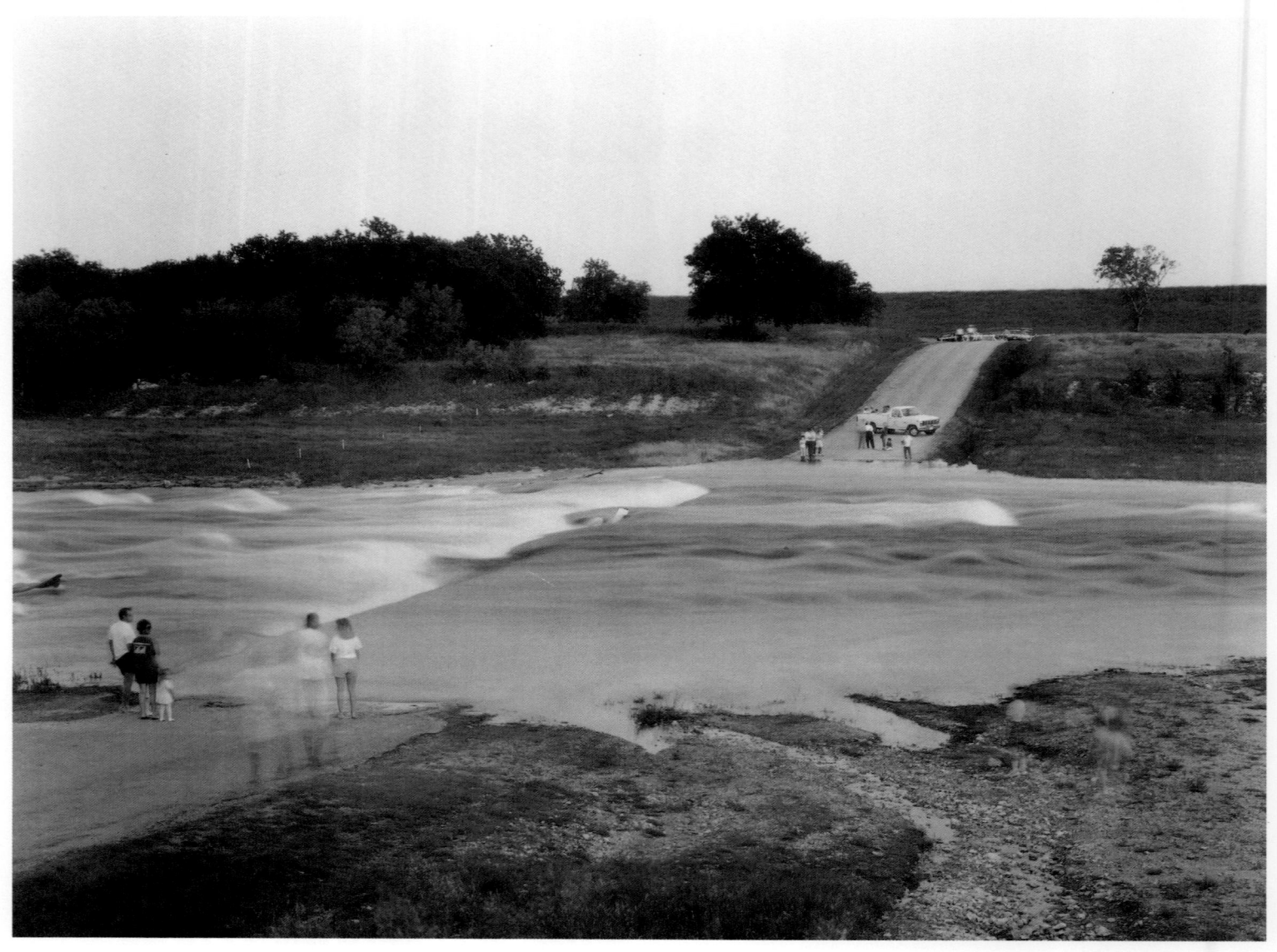

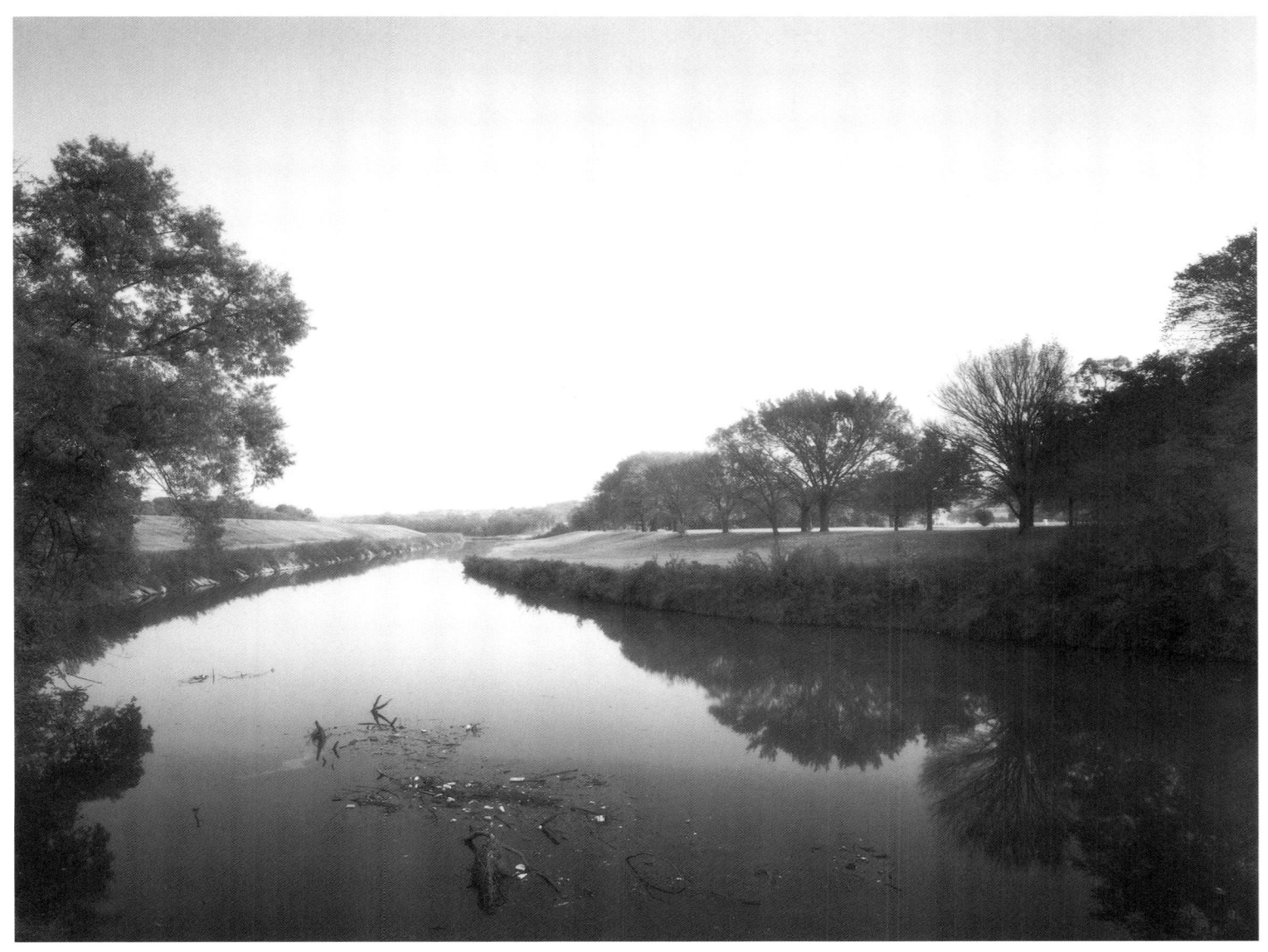

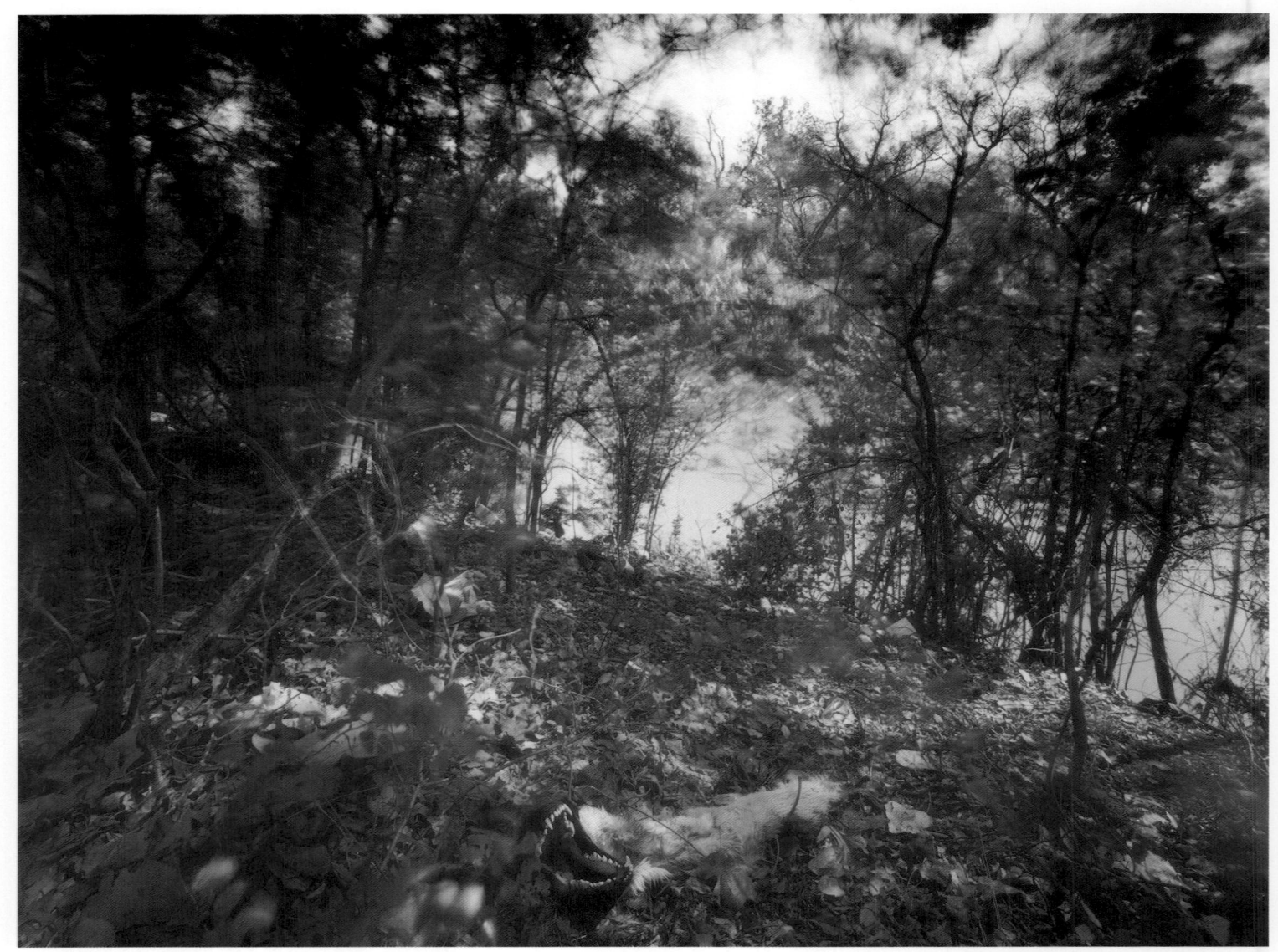

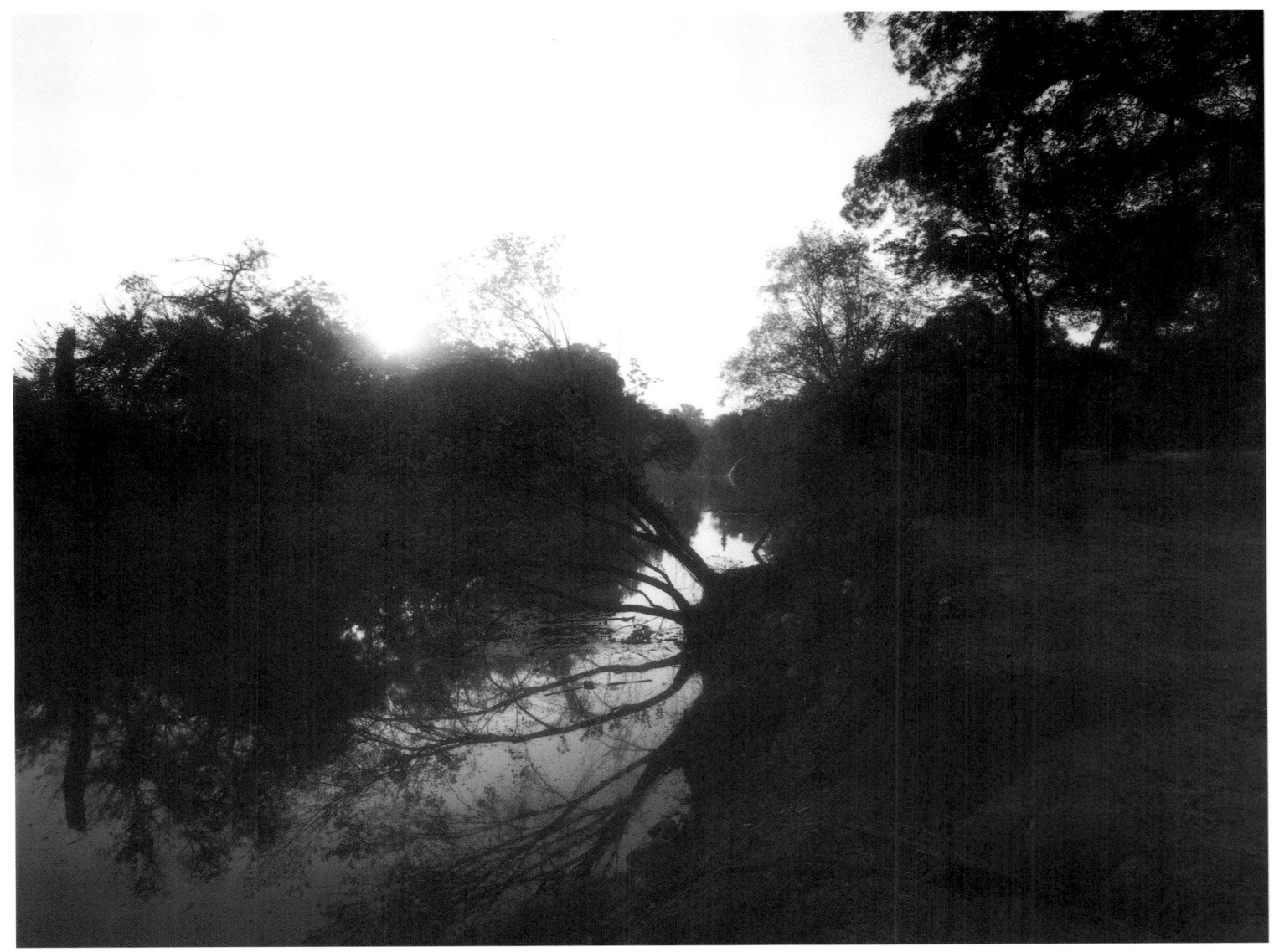

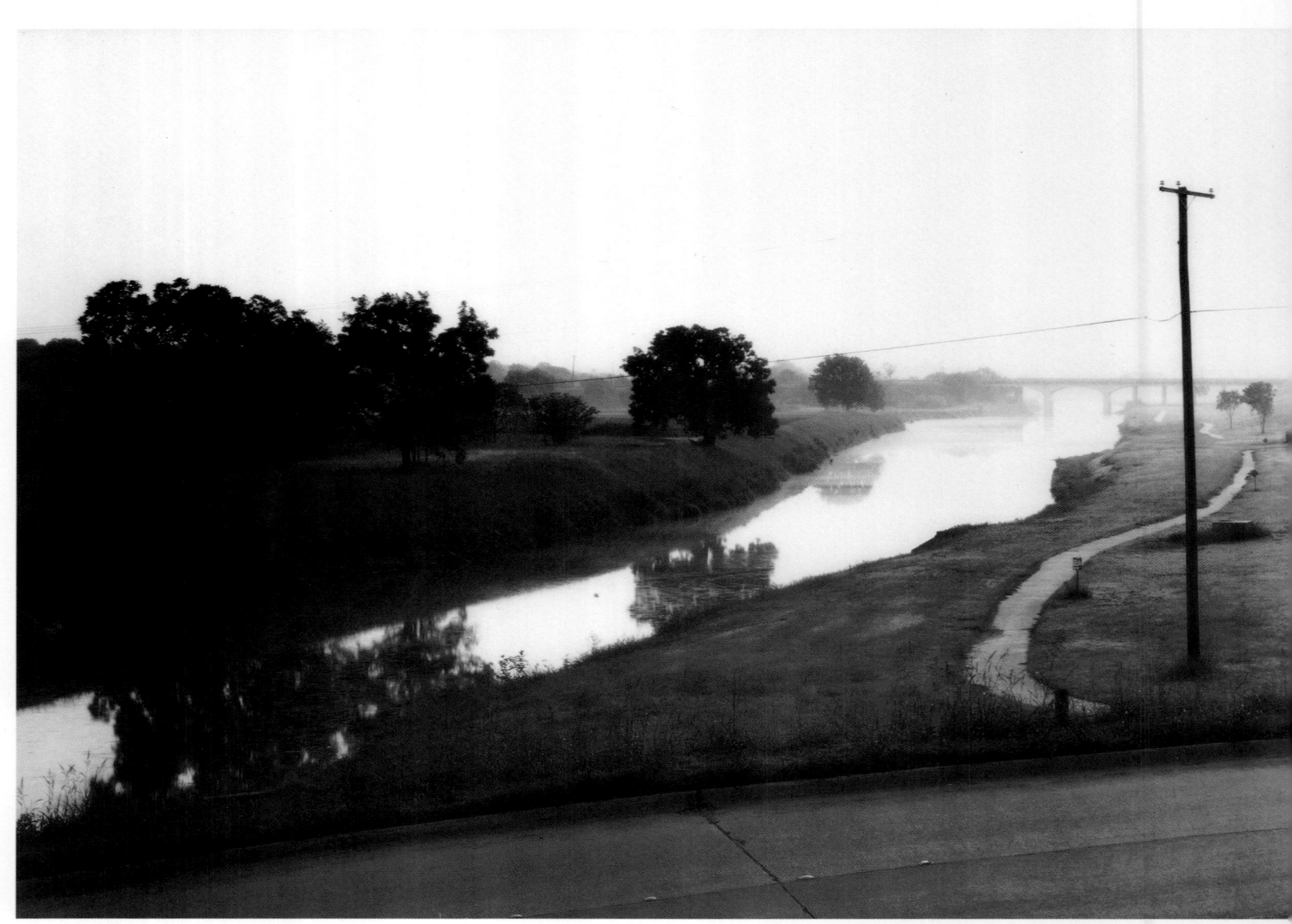

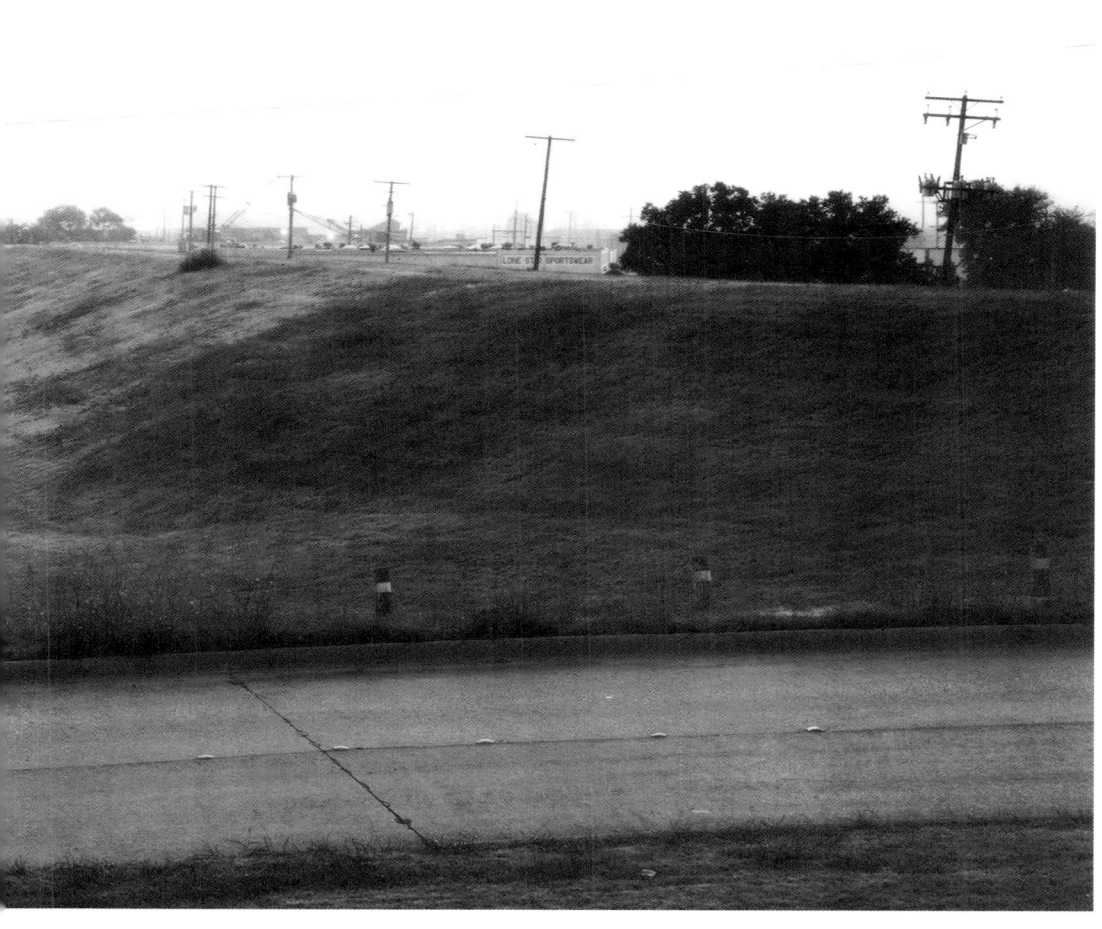

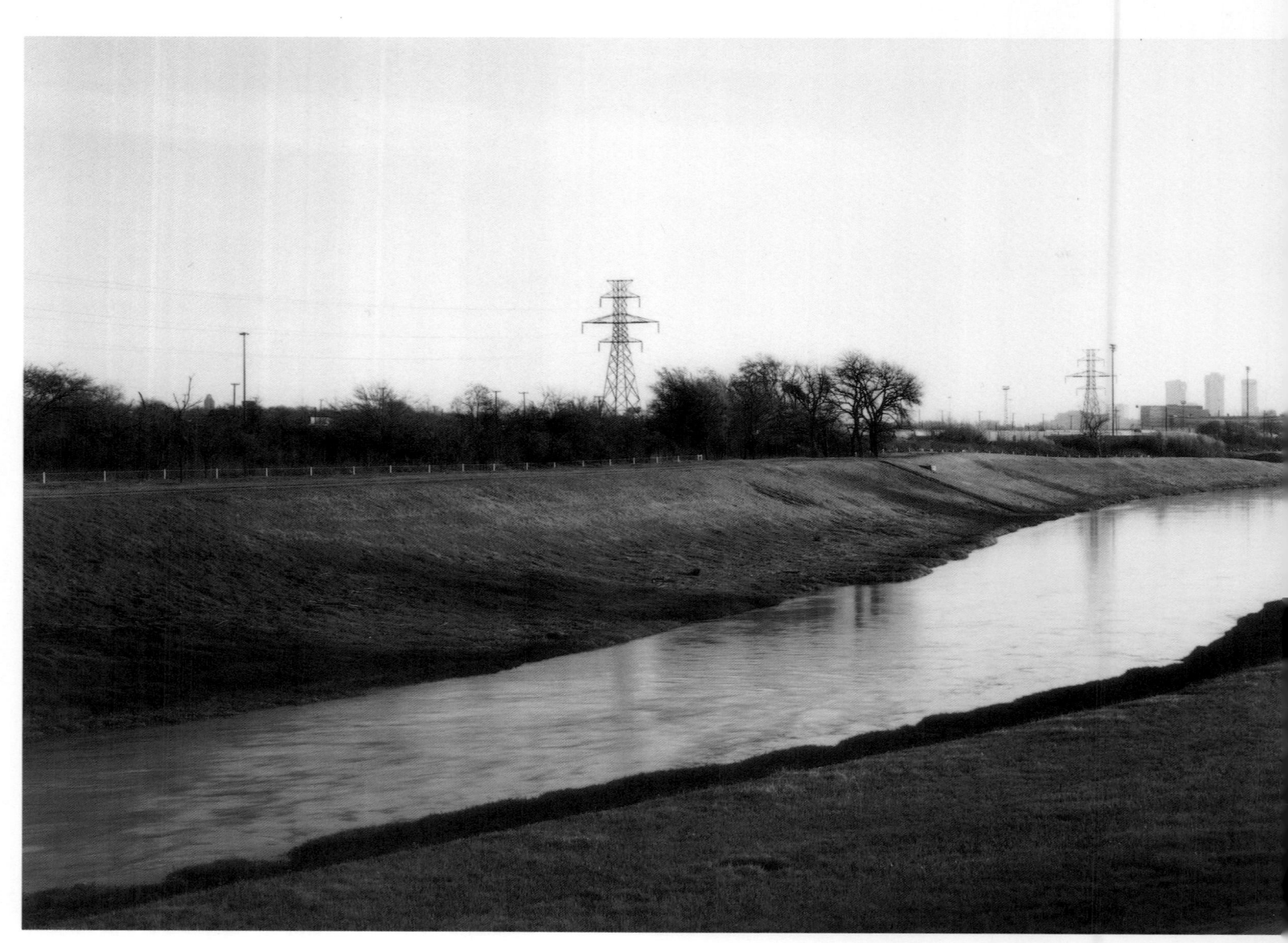

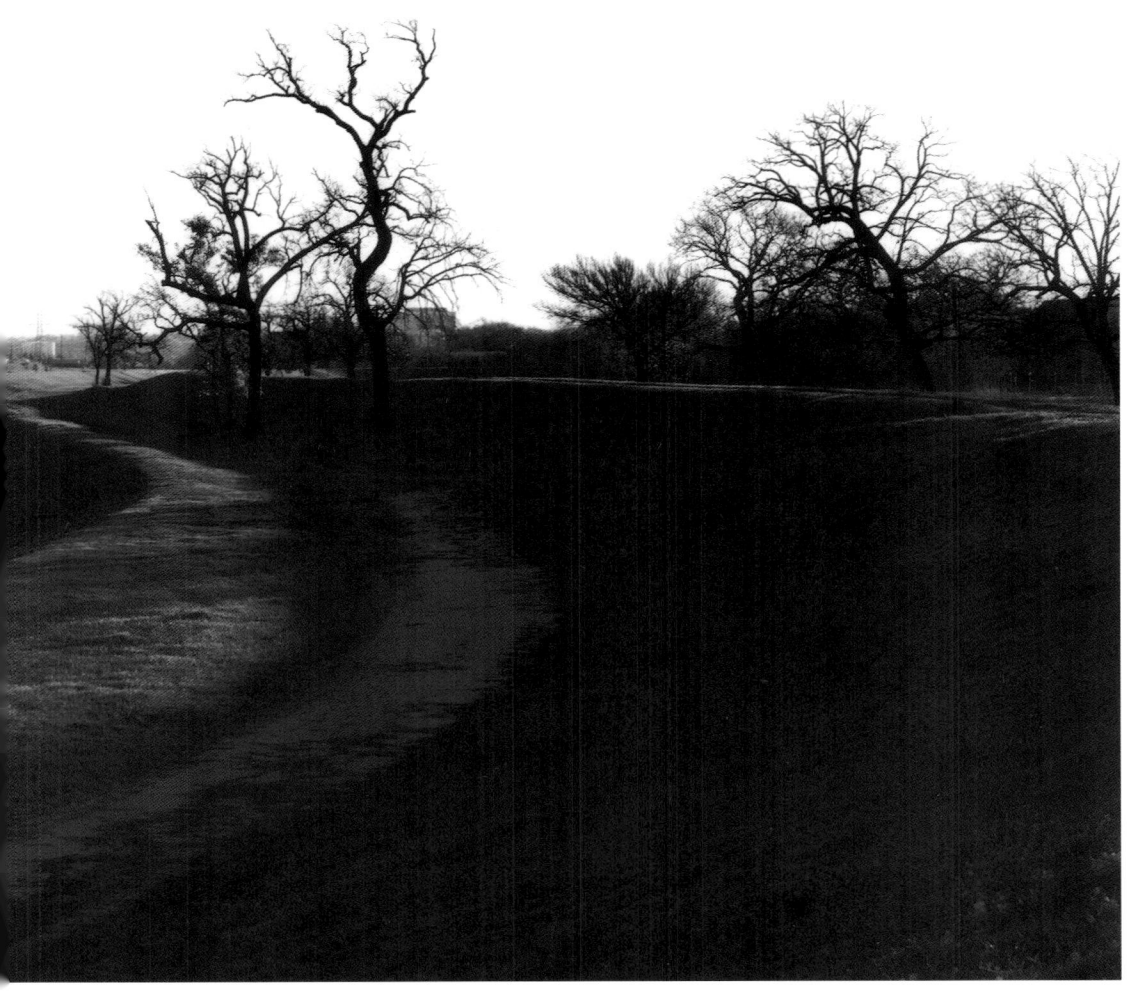

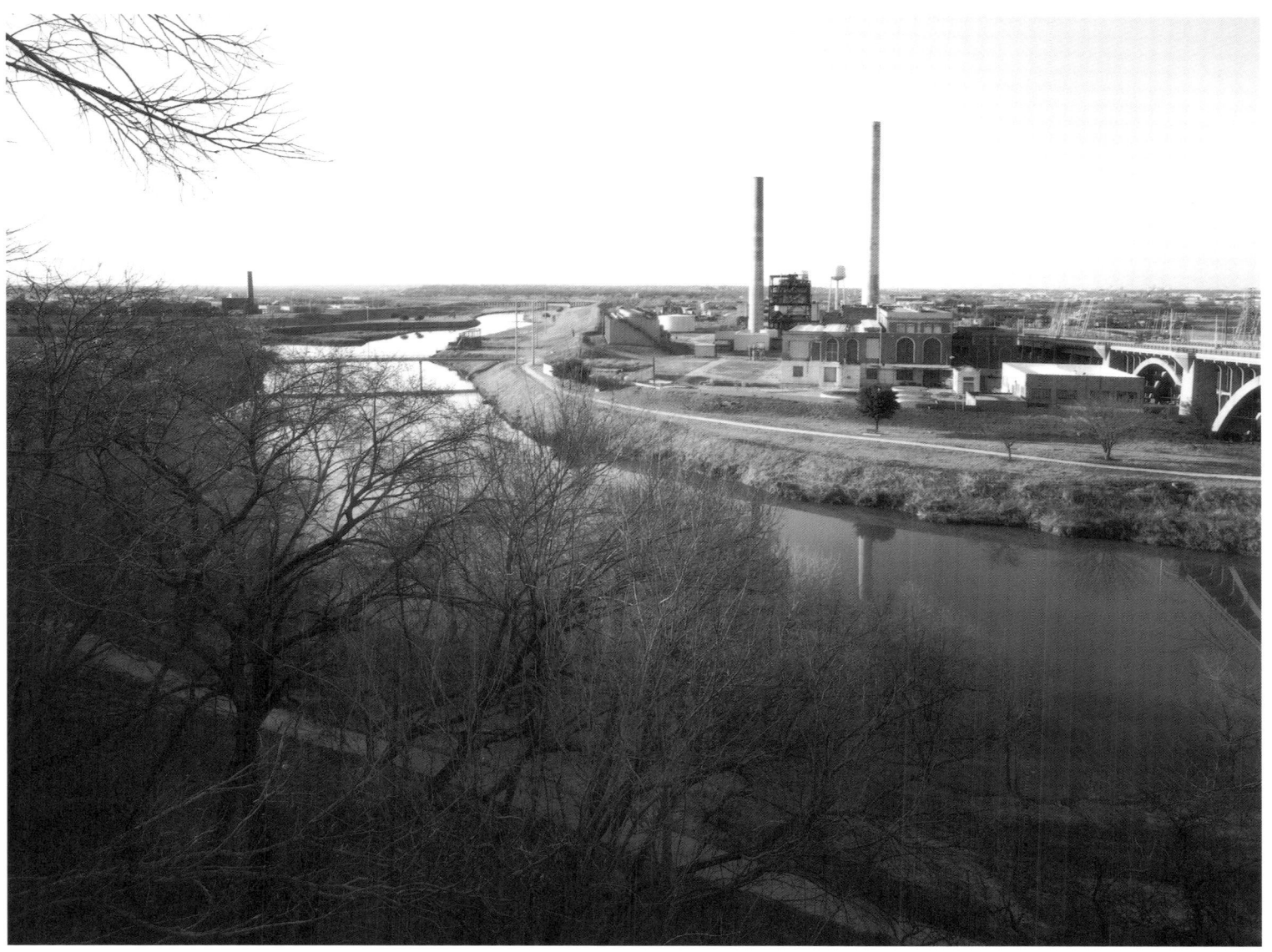

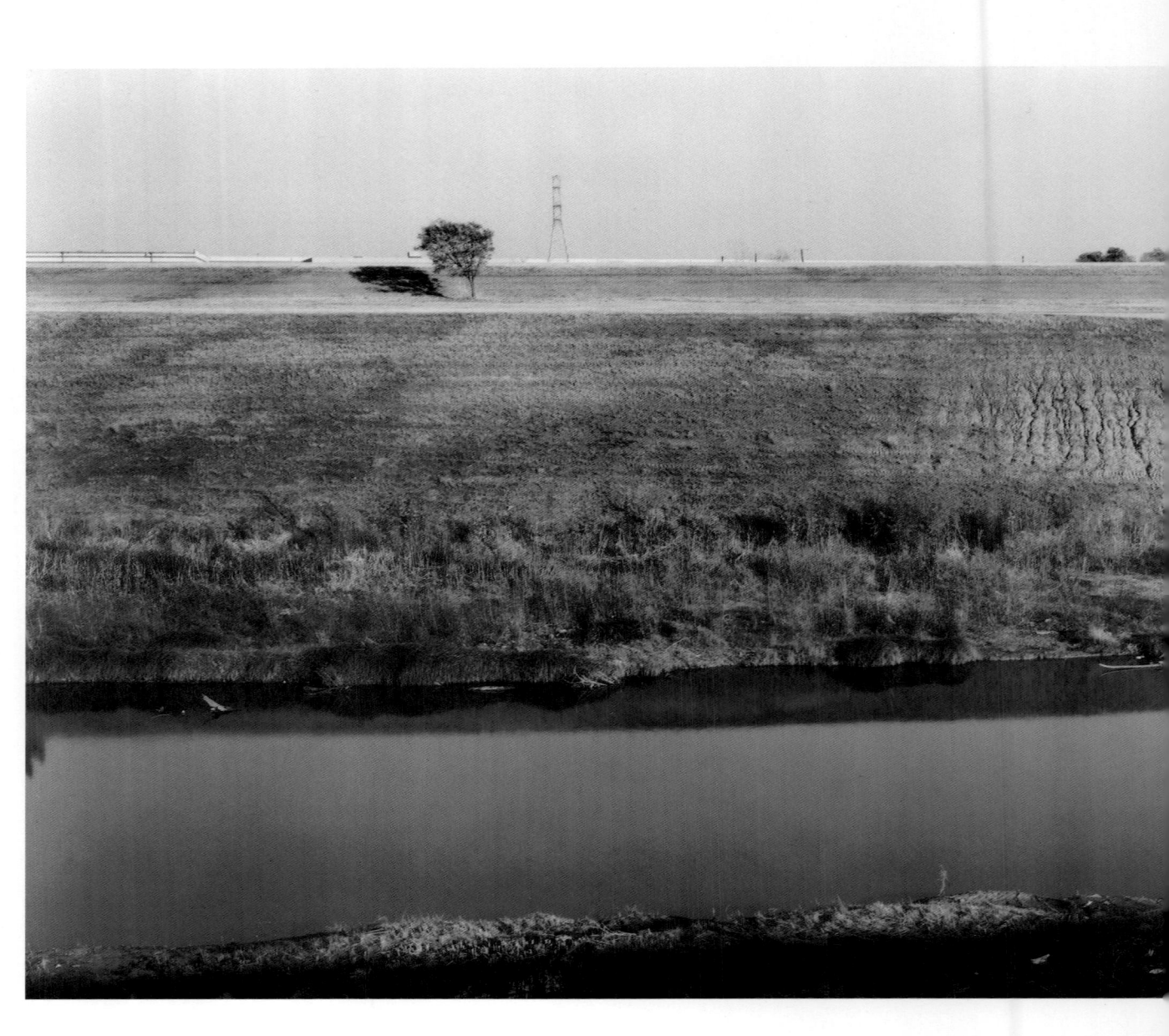

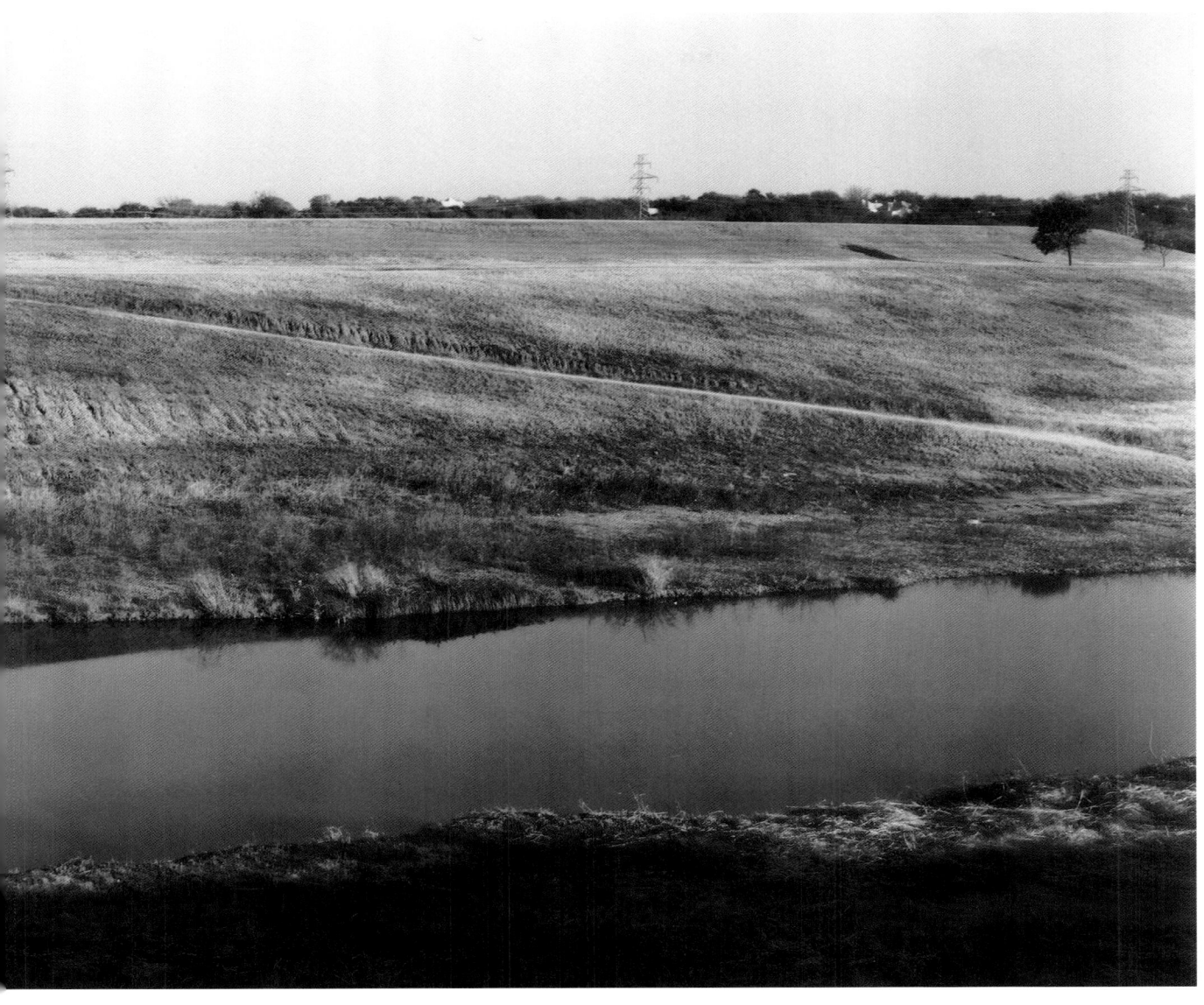

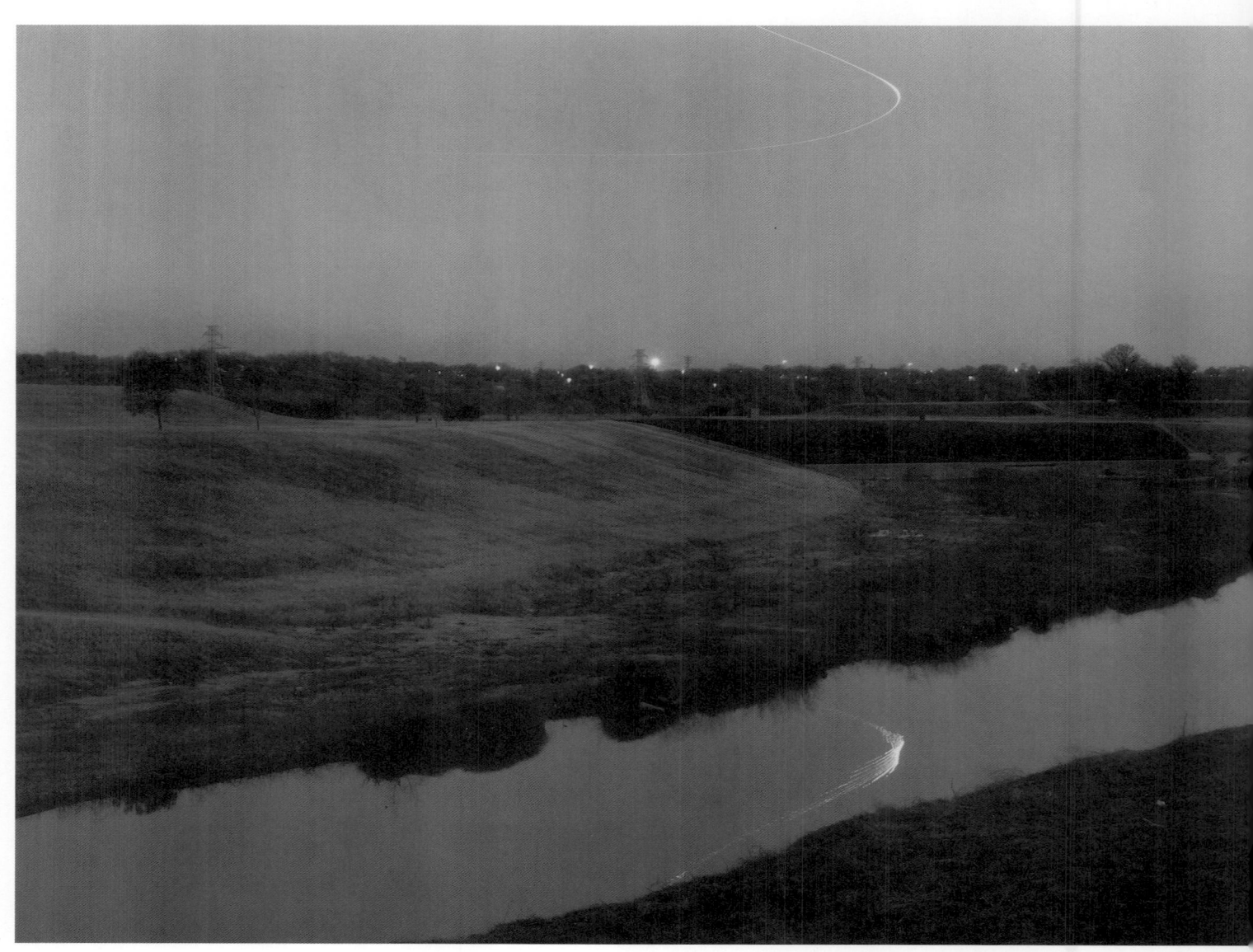

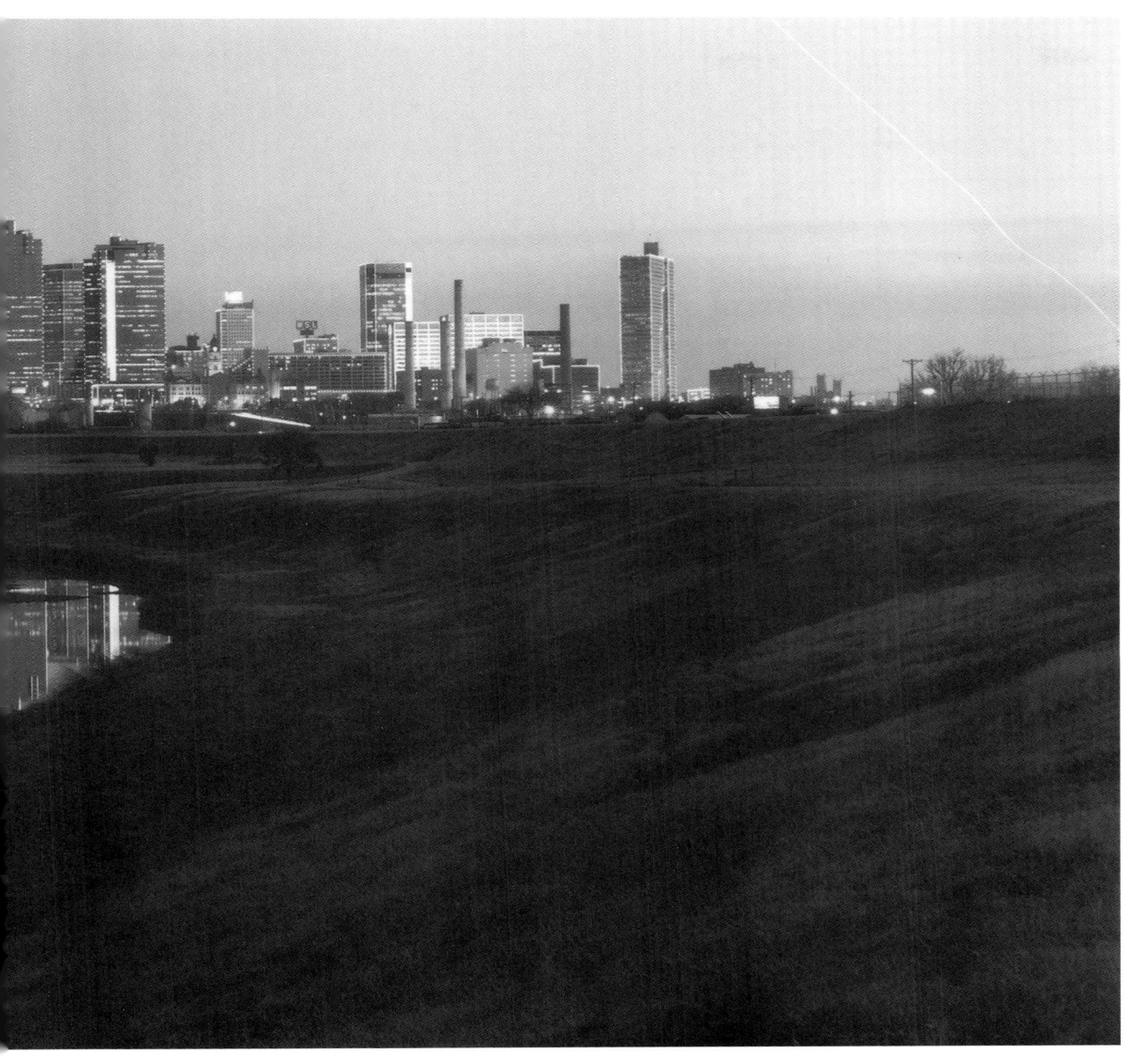

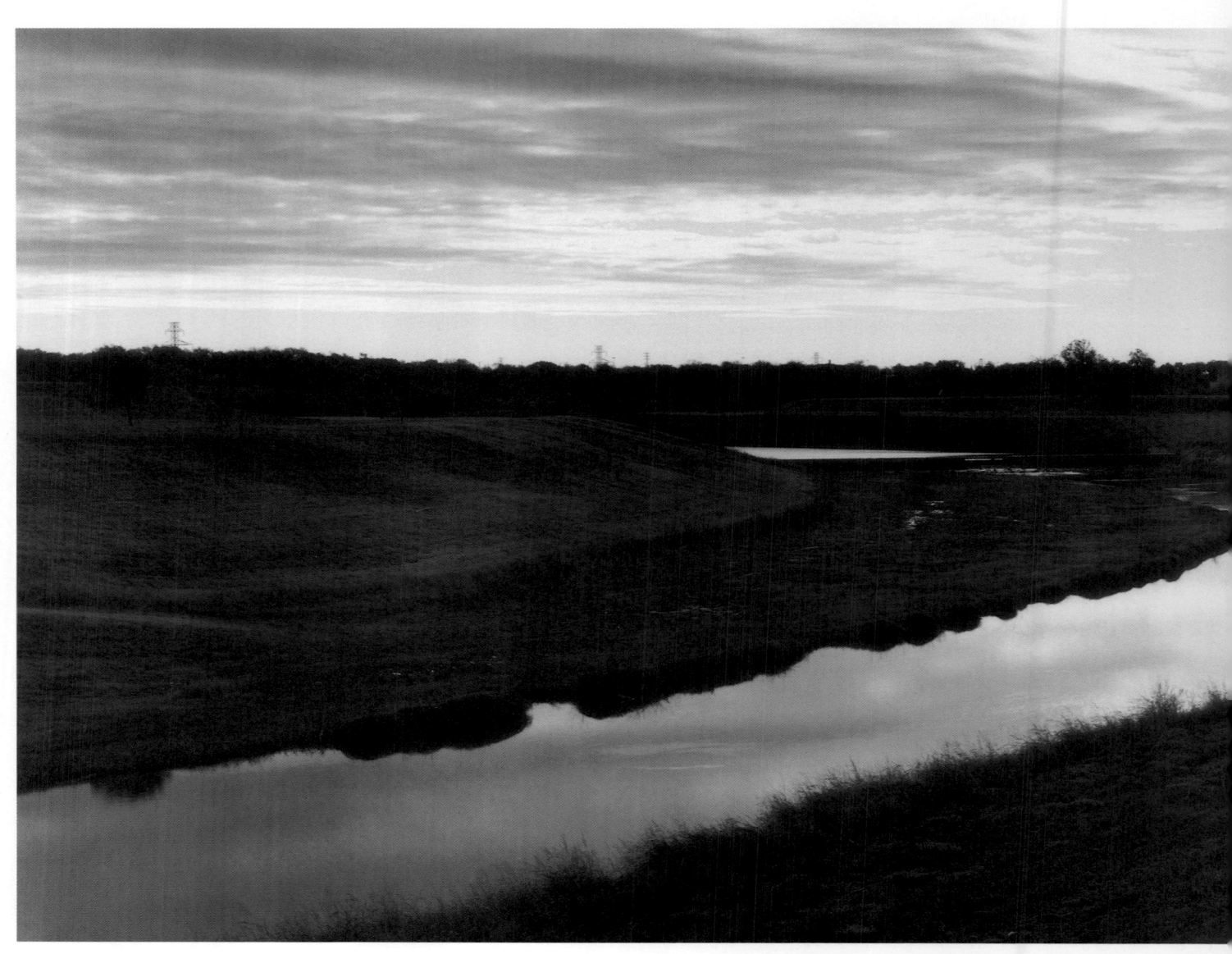

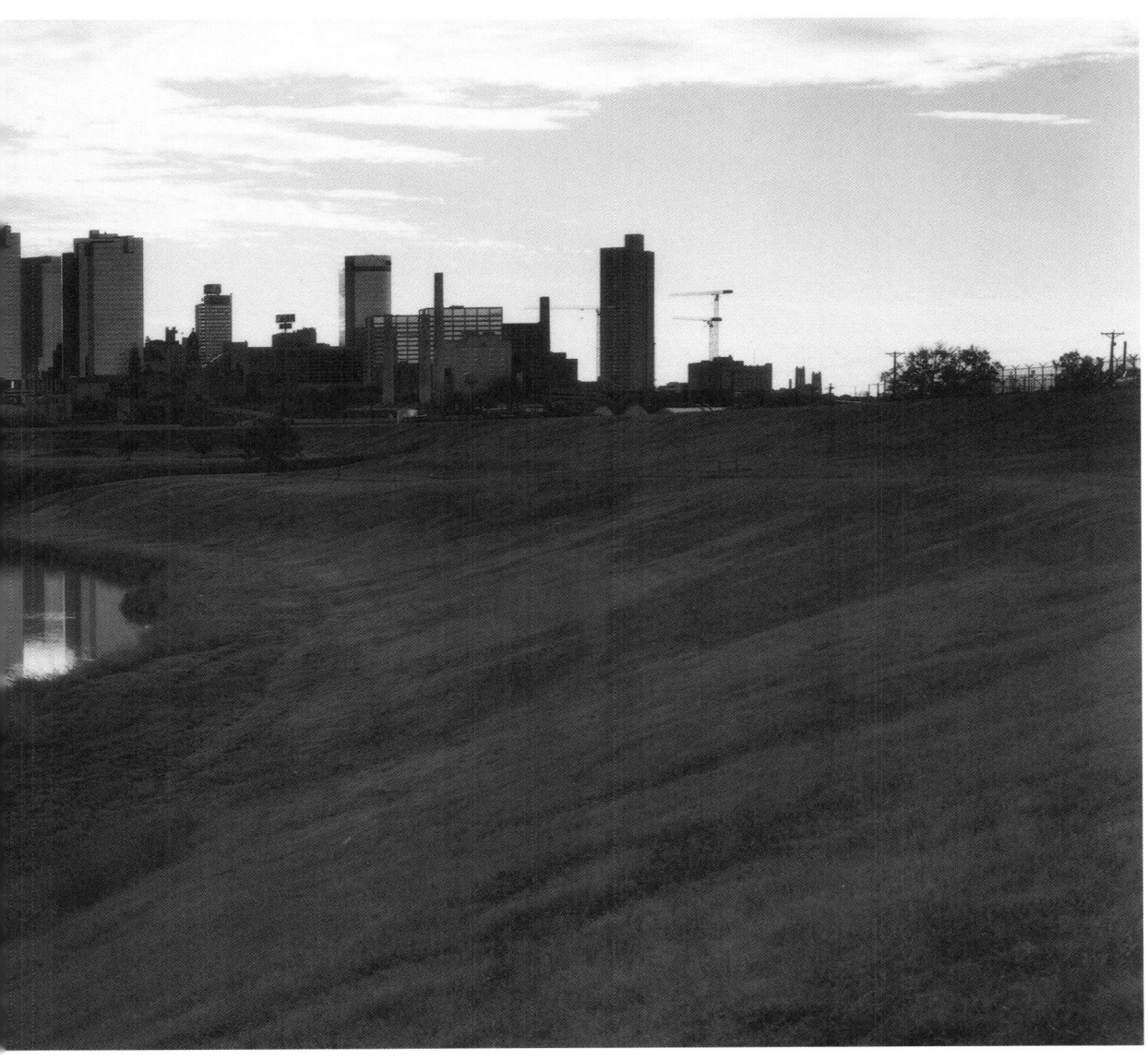

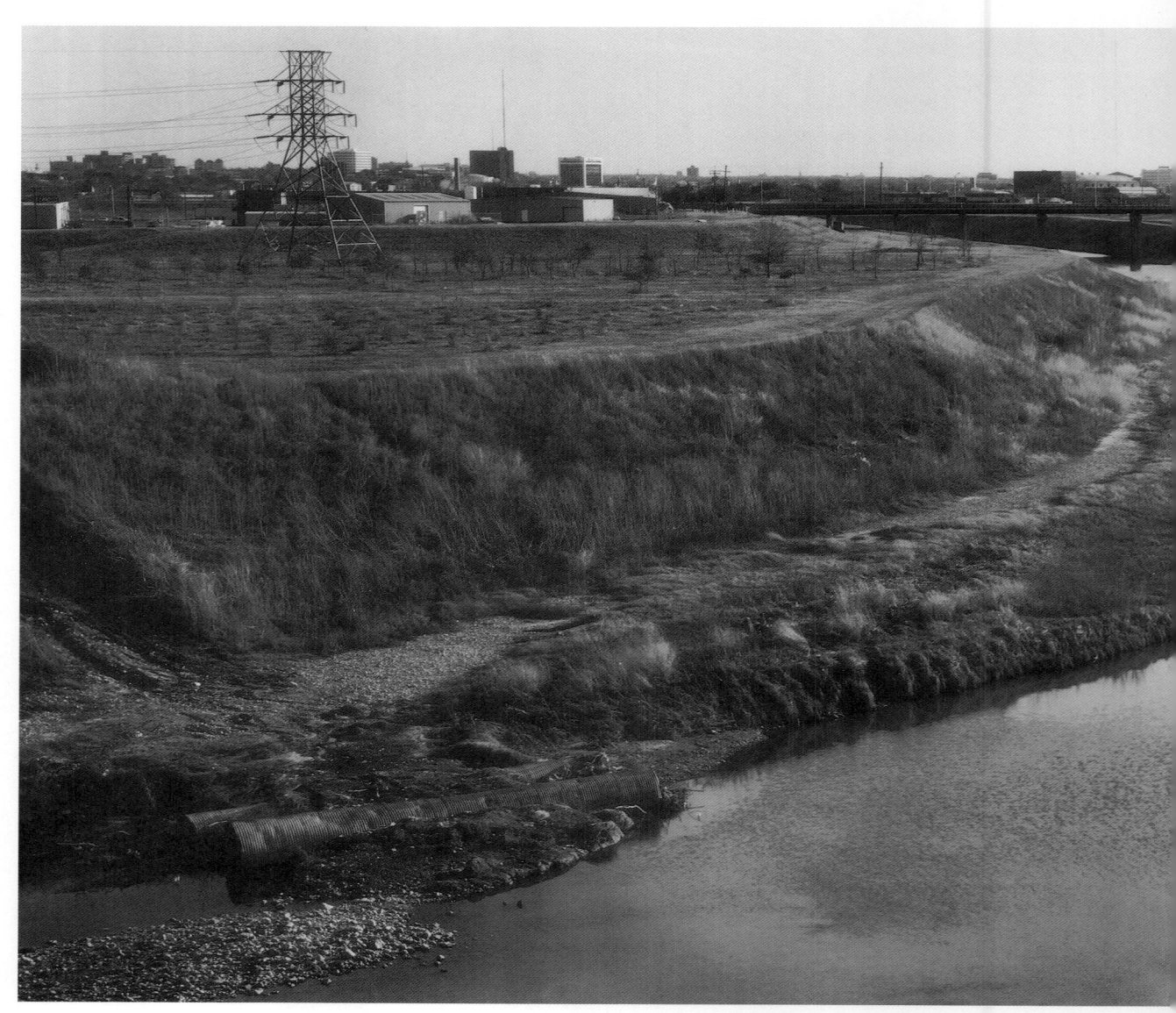

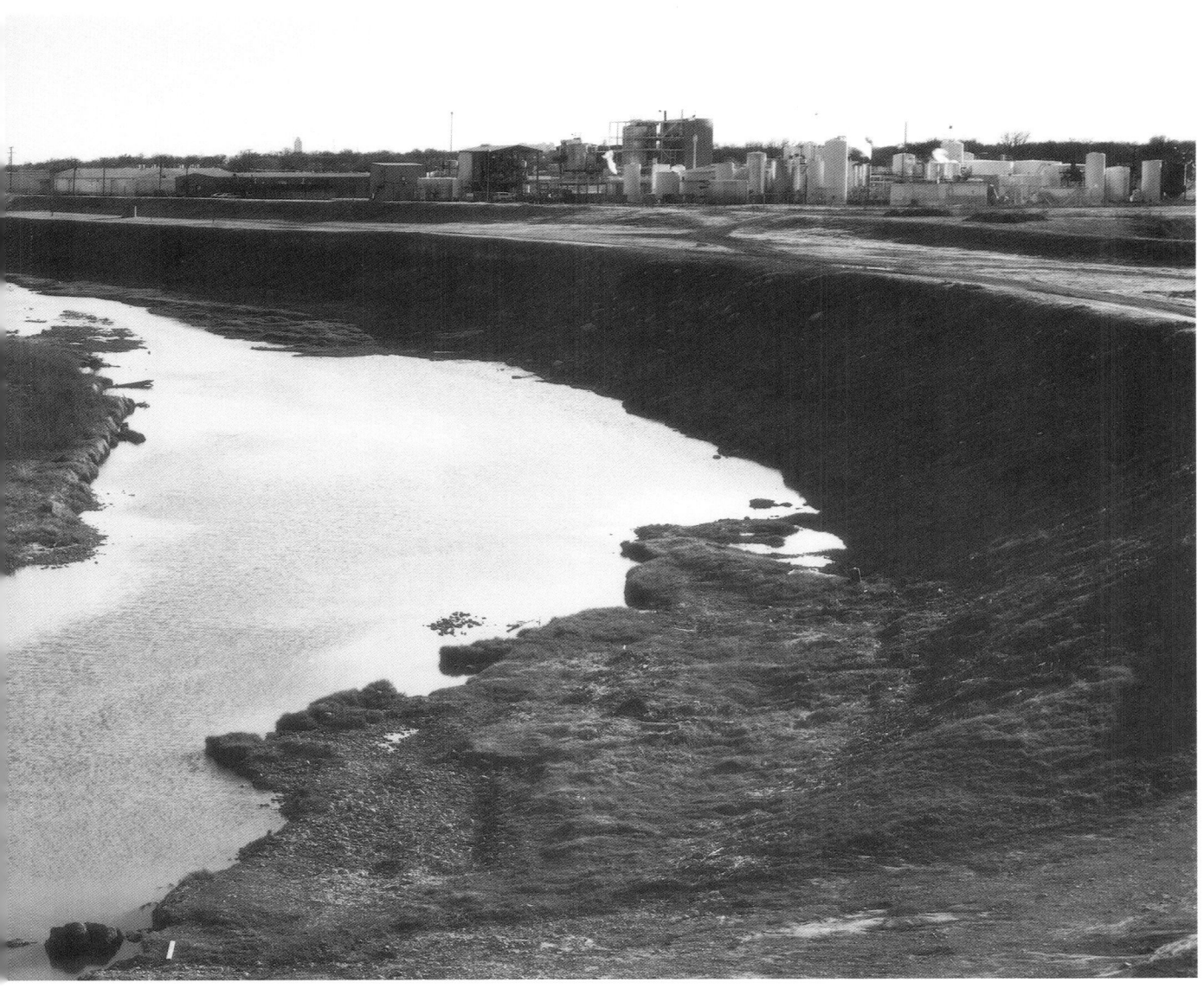

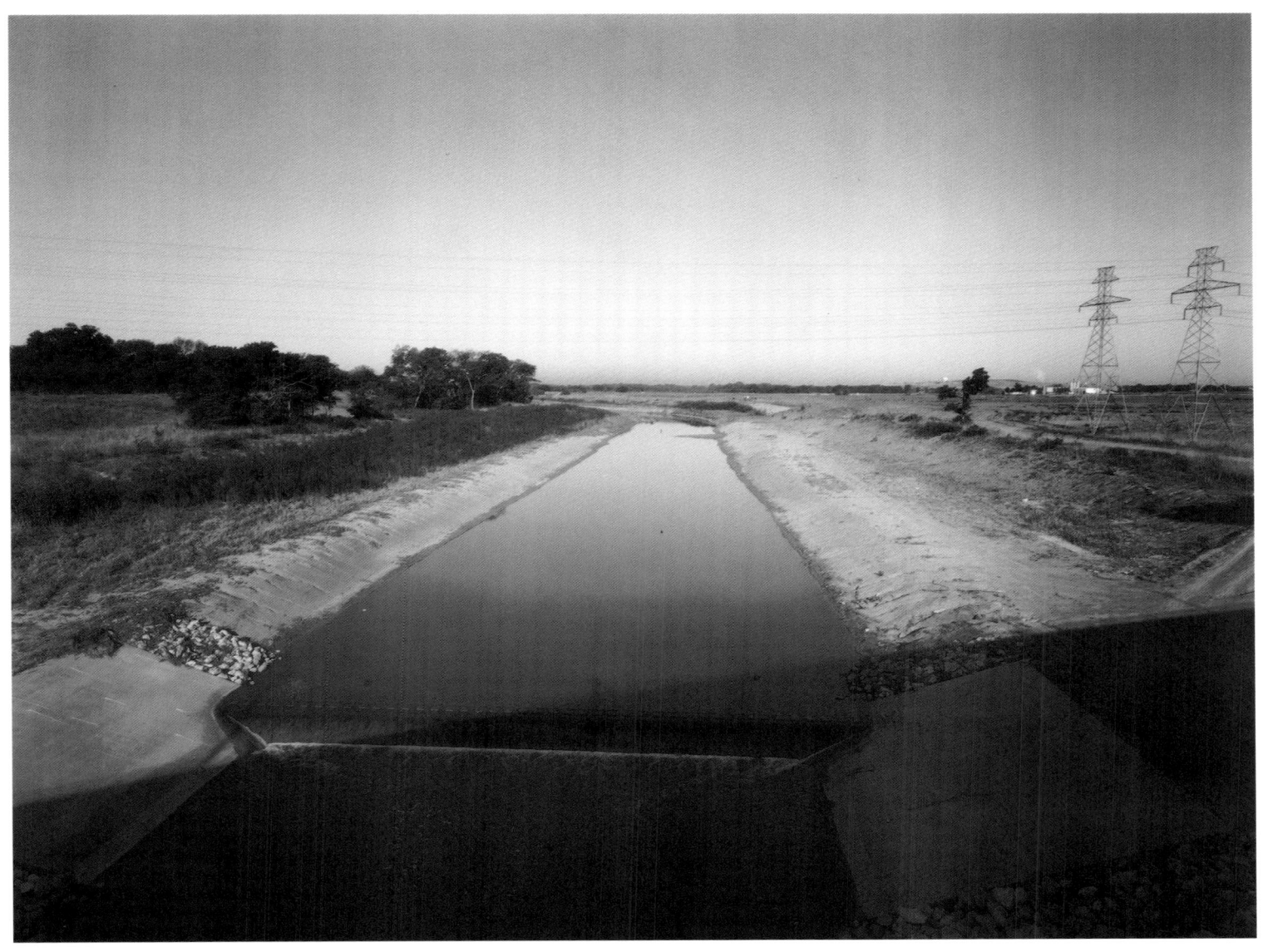

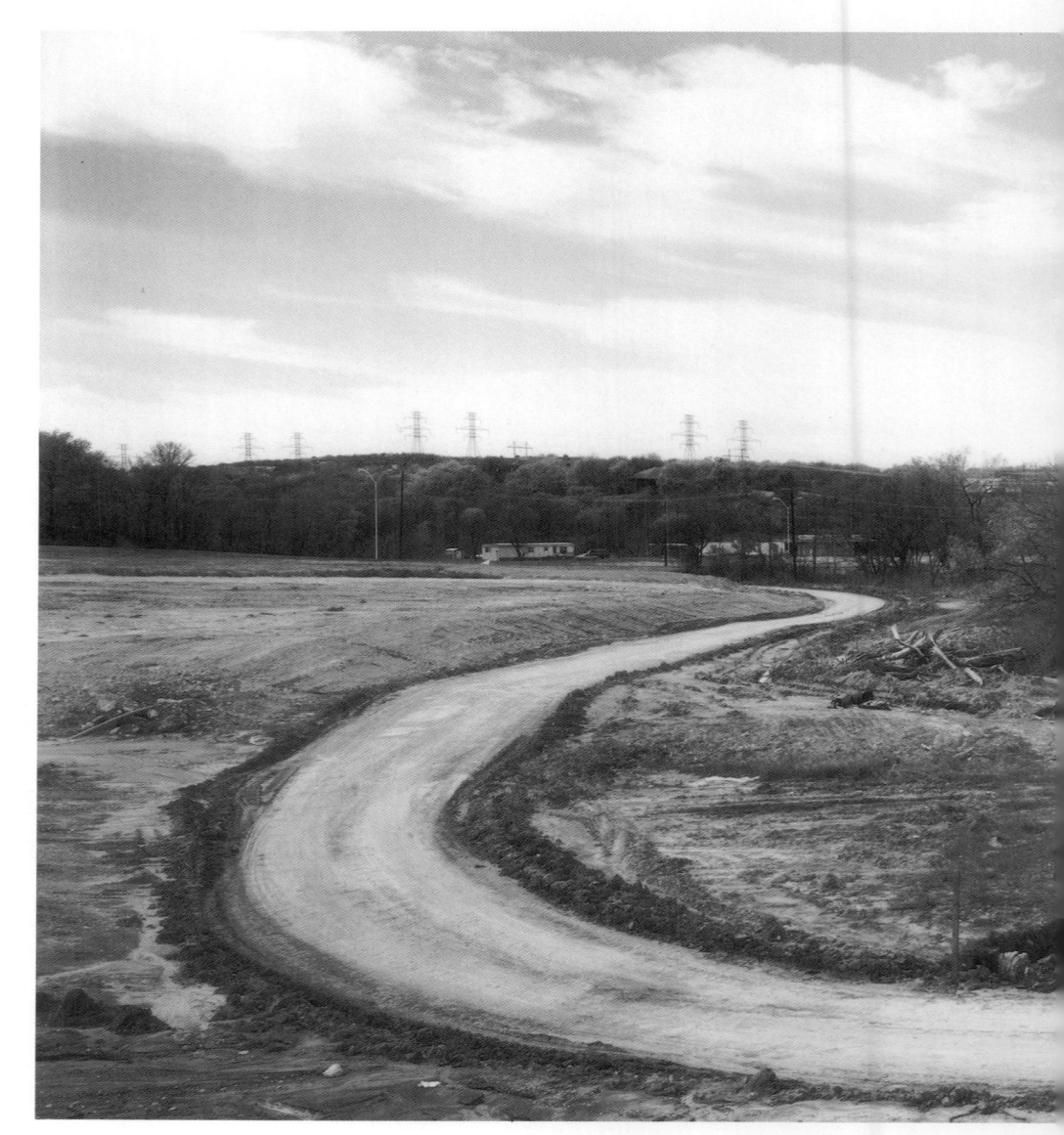

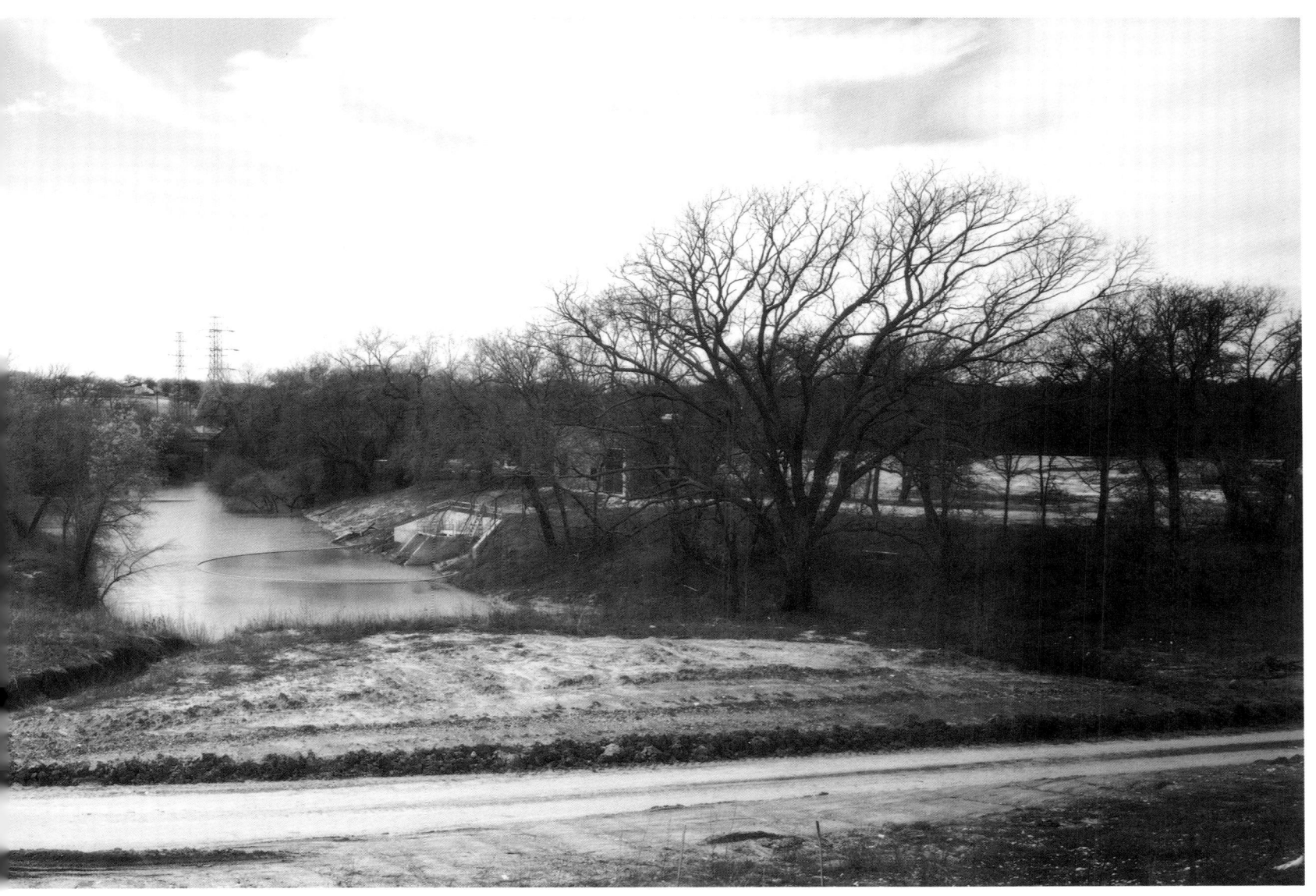

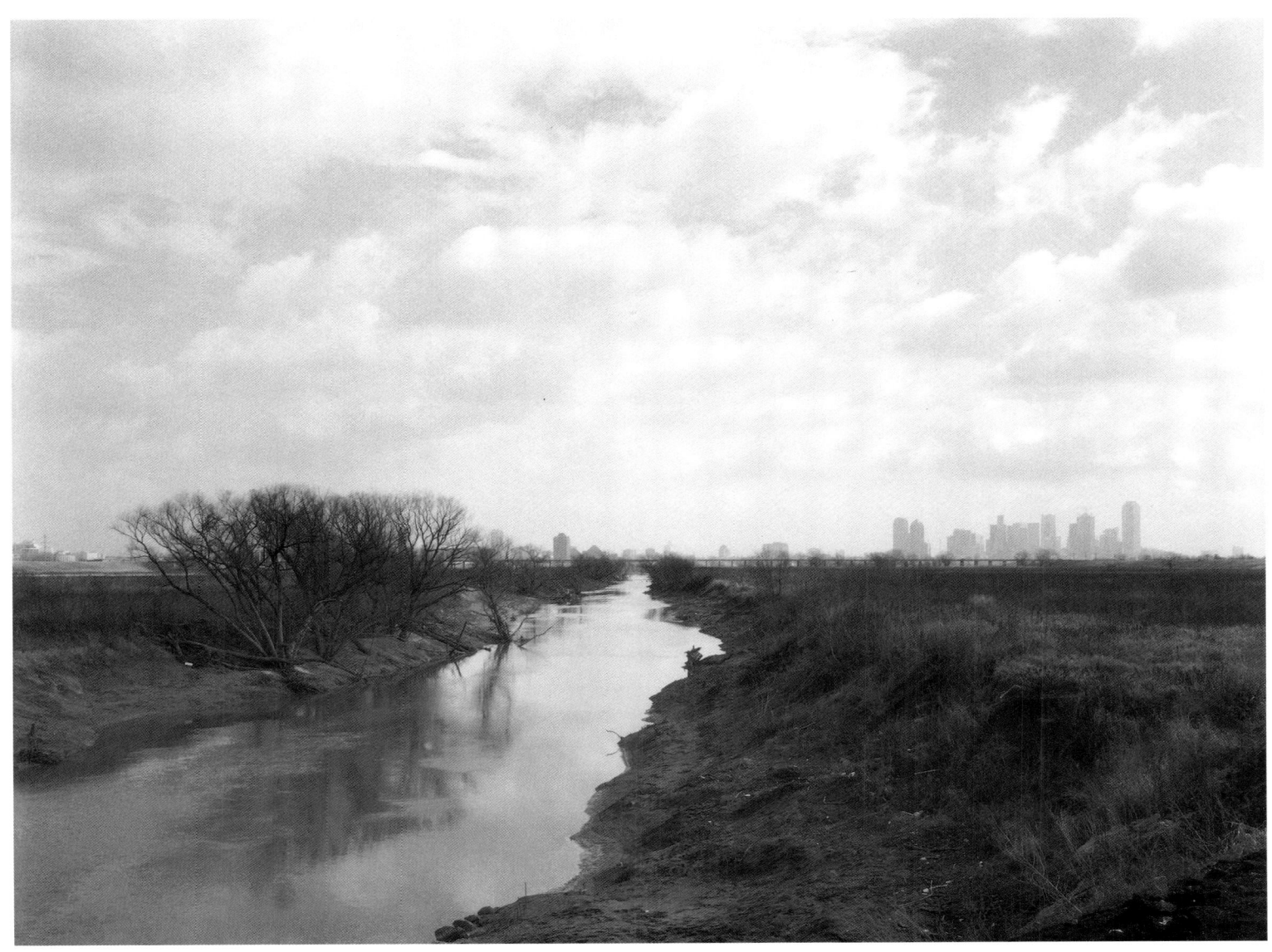

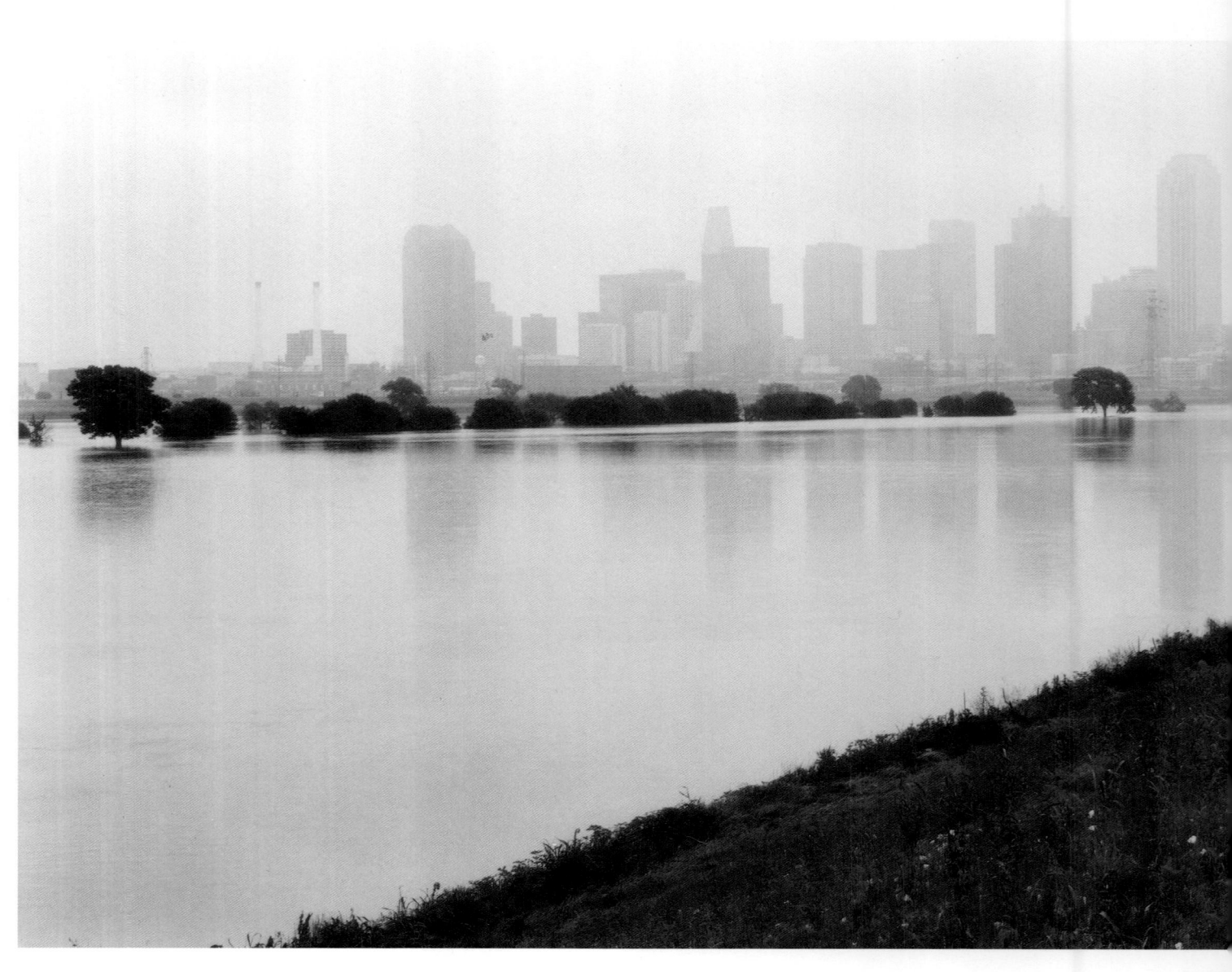

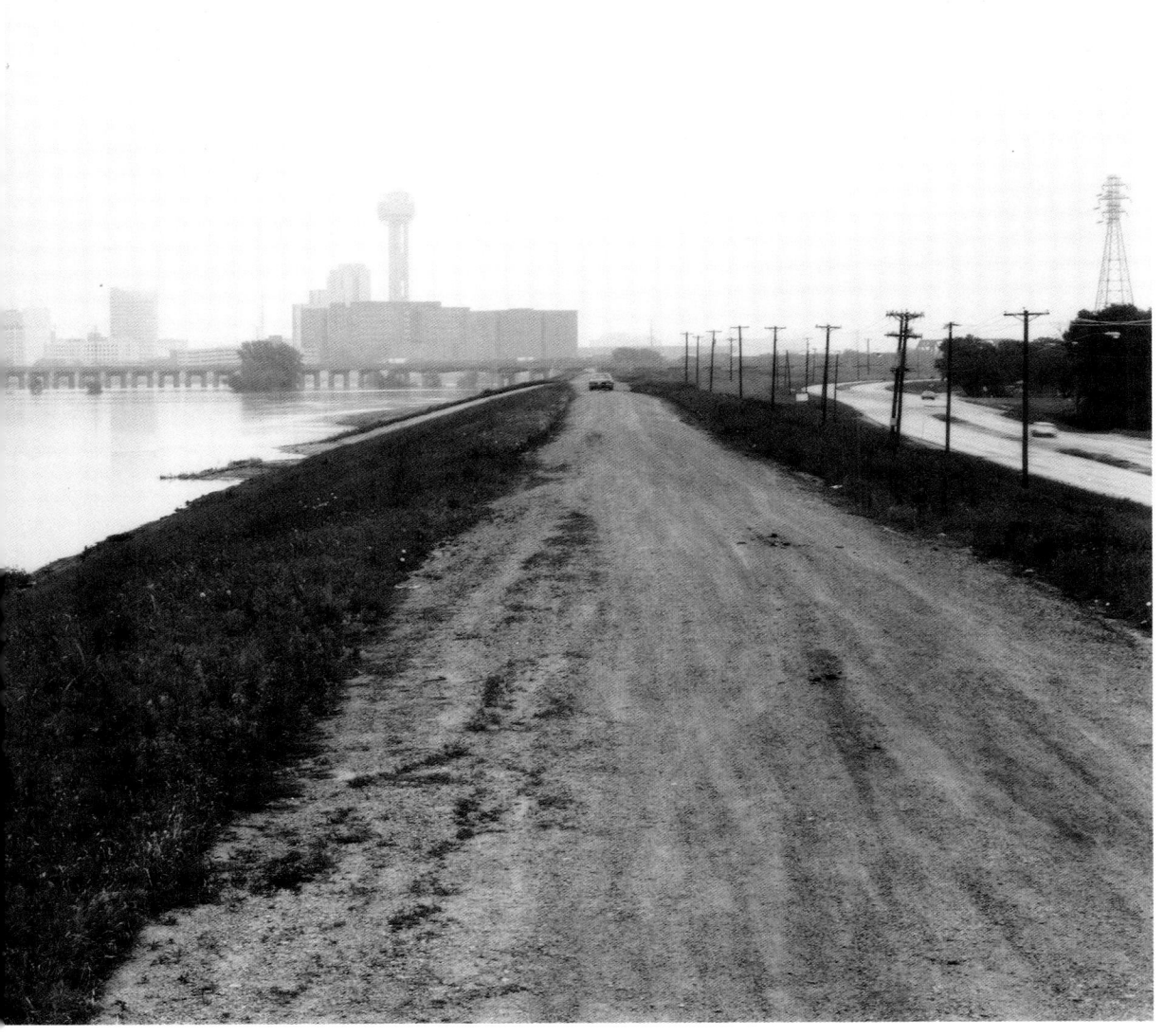

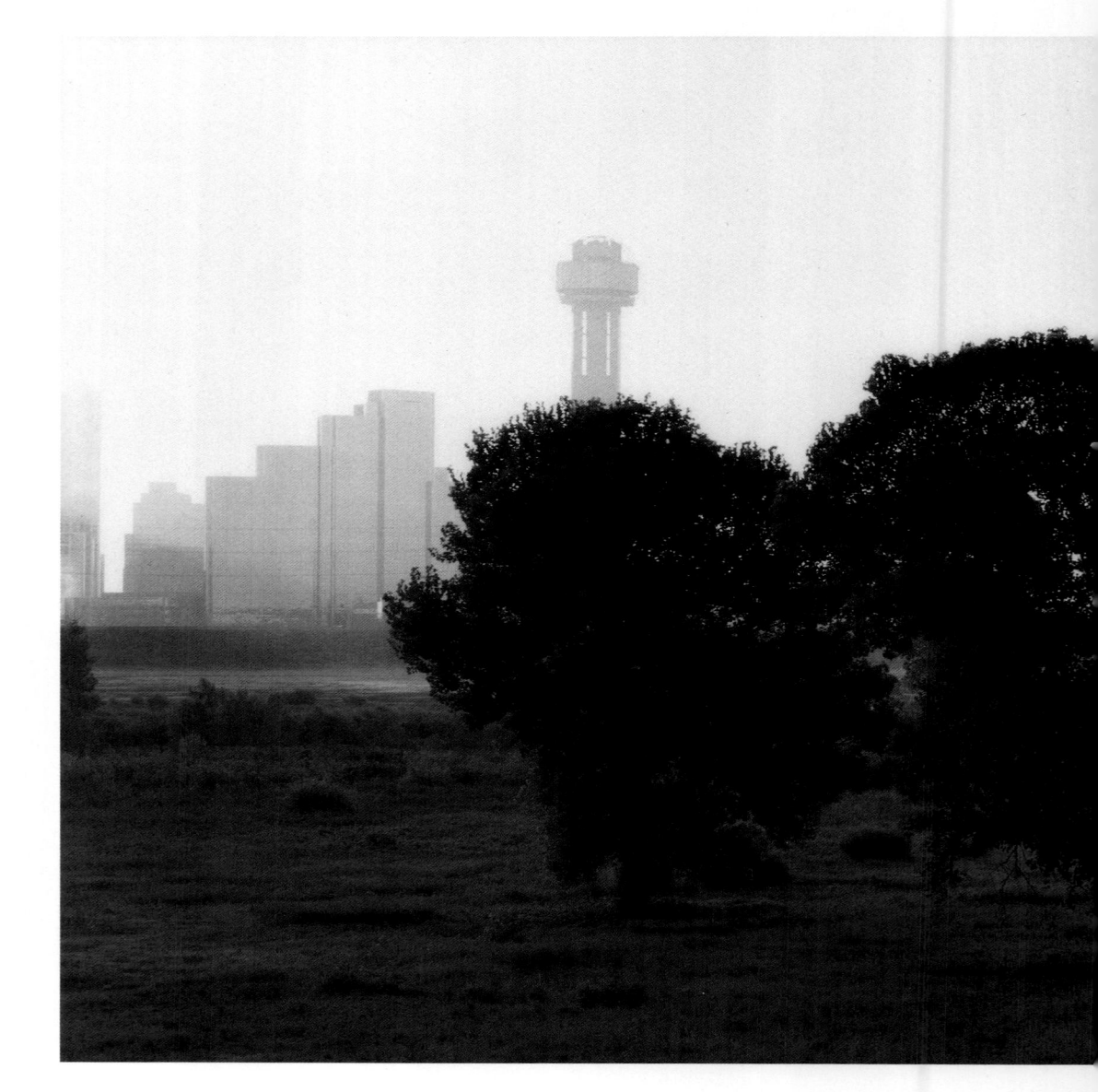

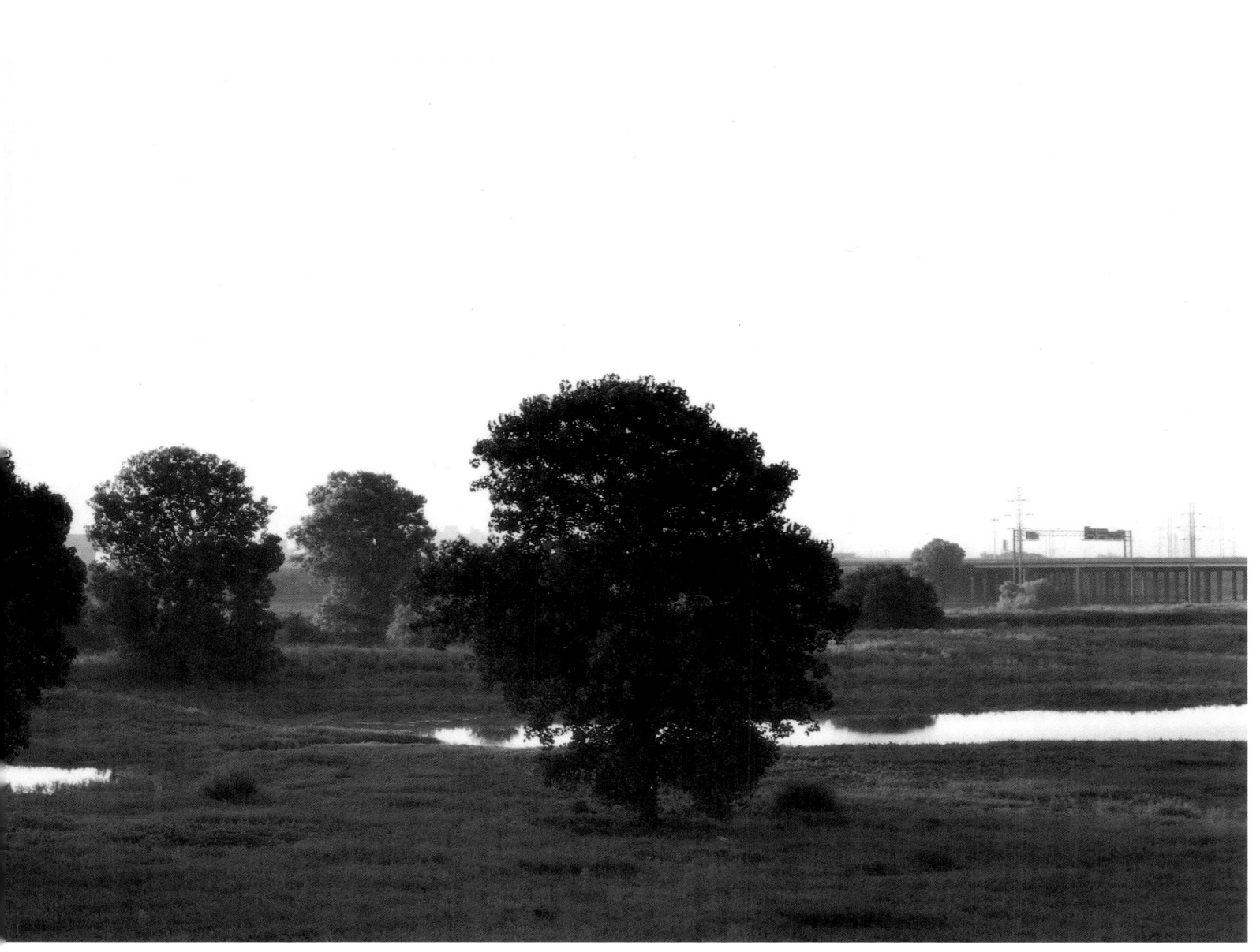

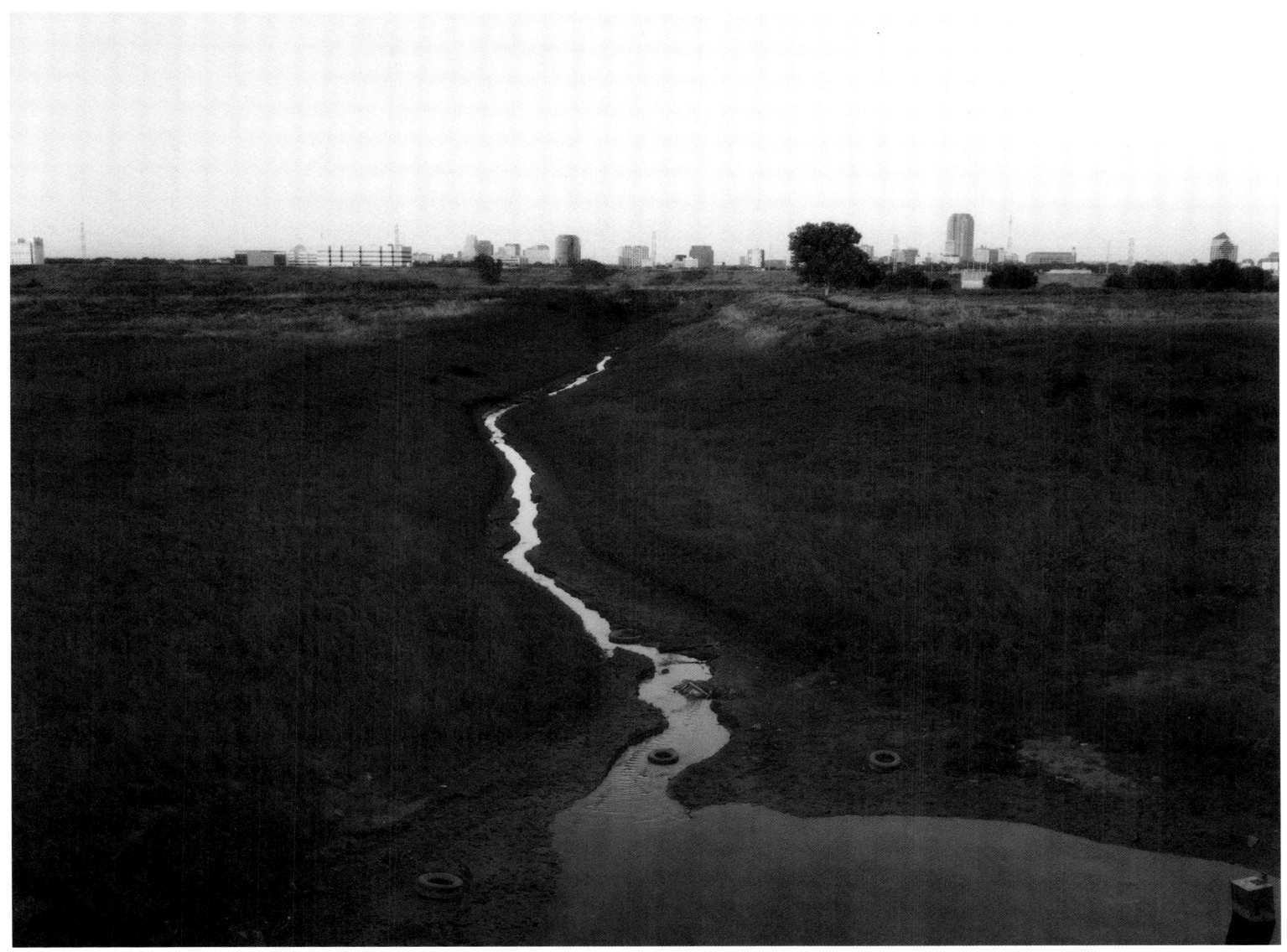

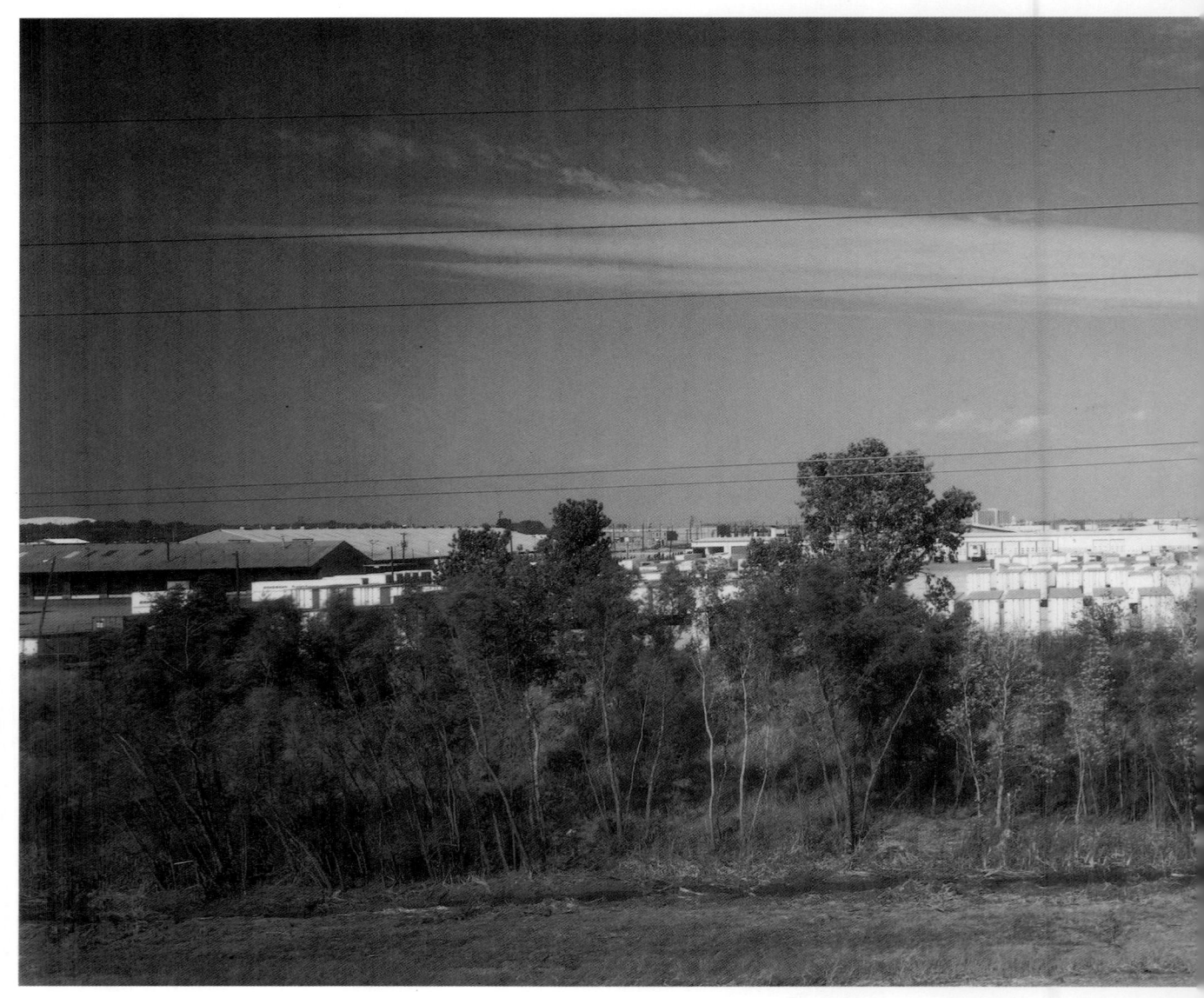

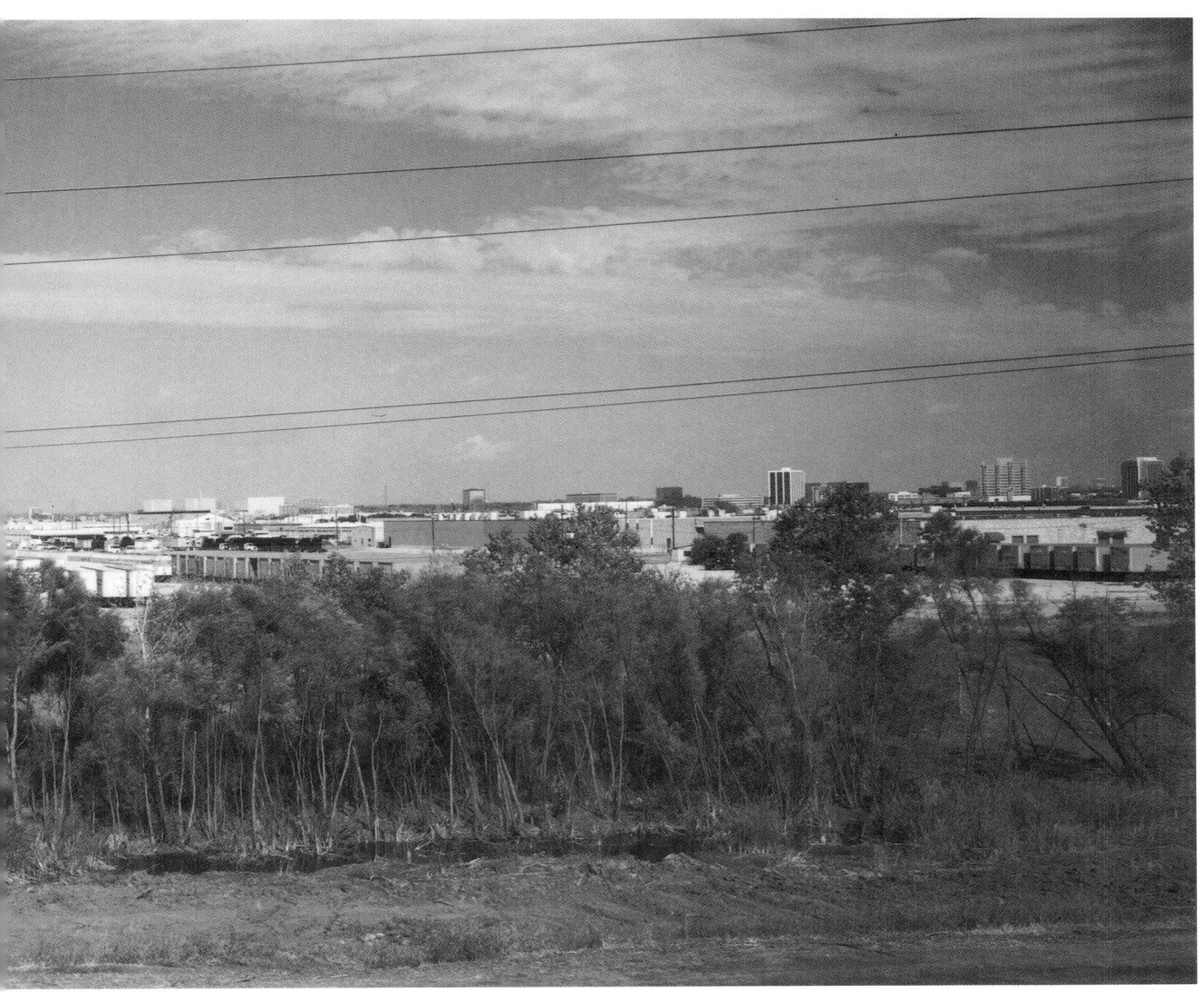

42

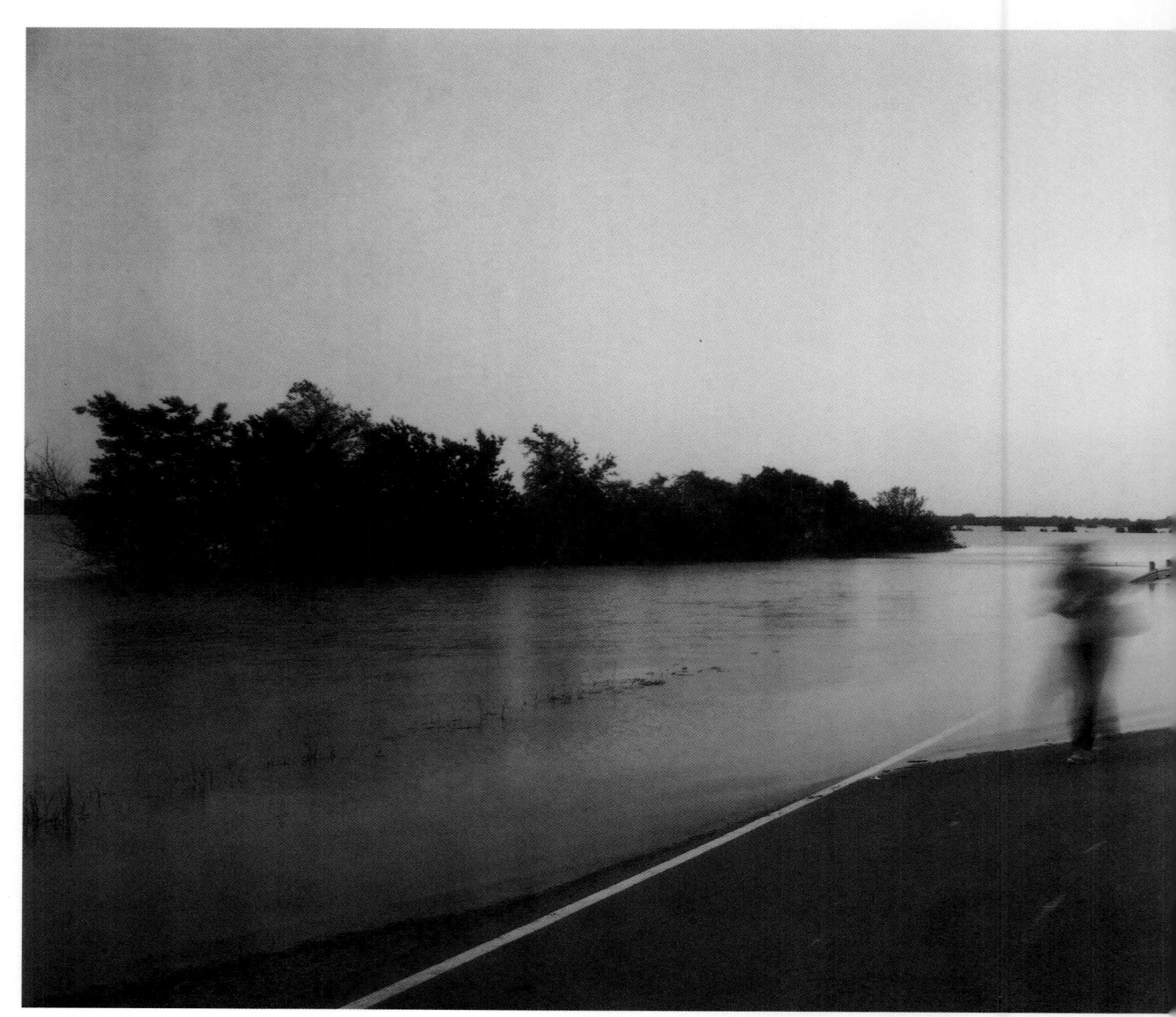

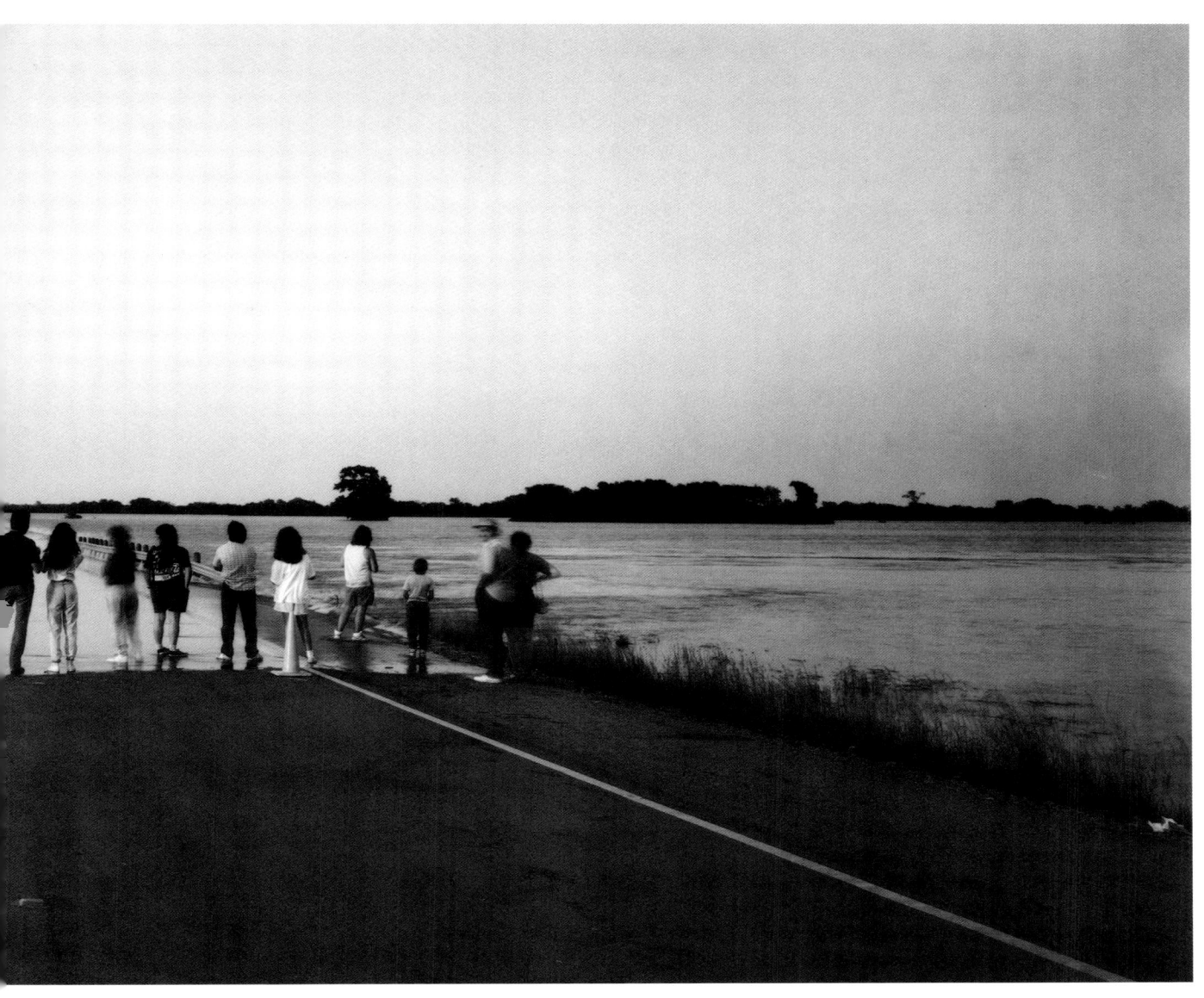

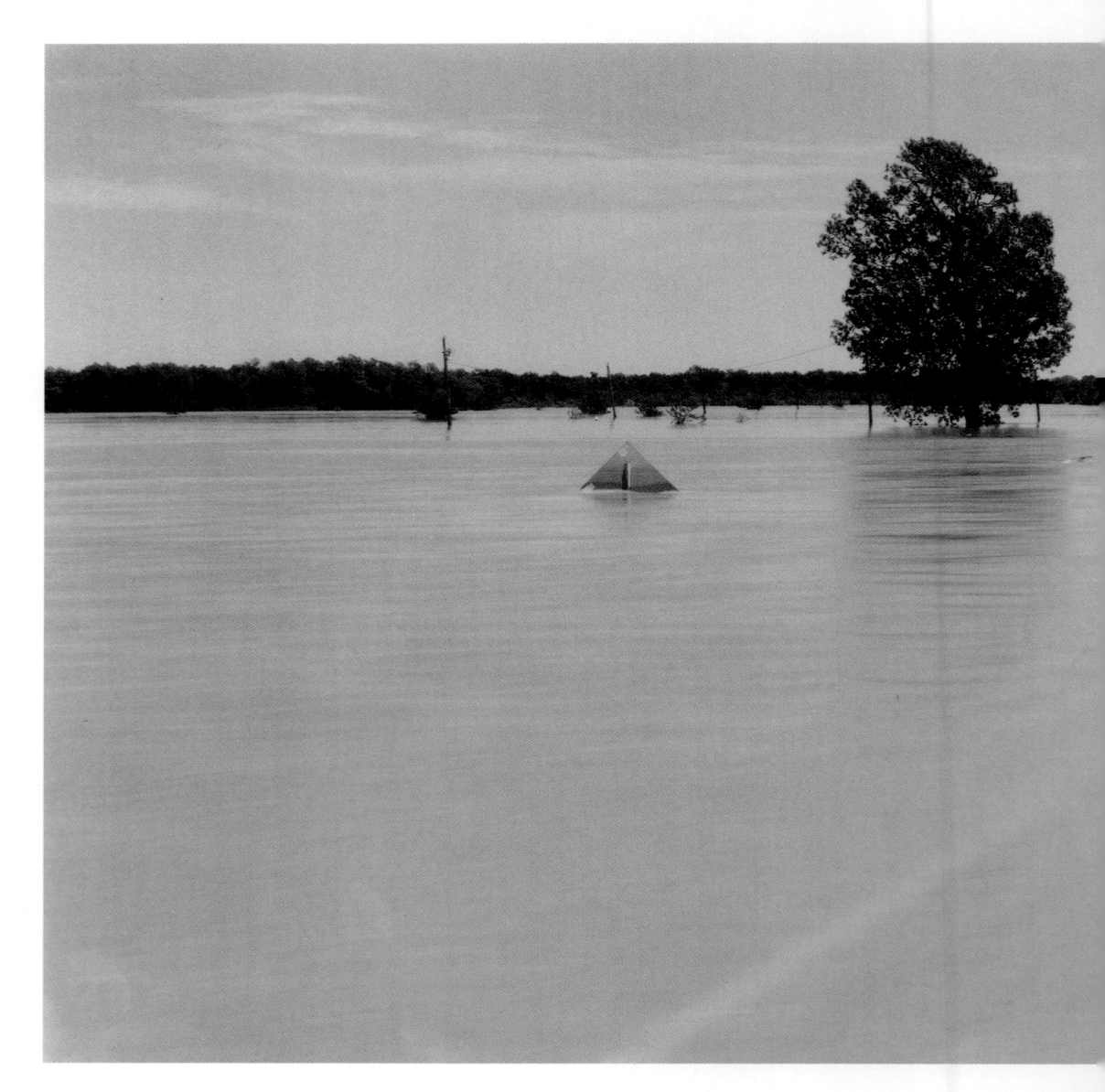

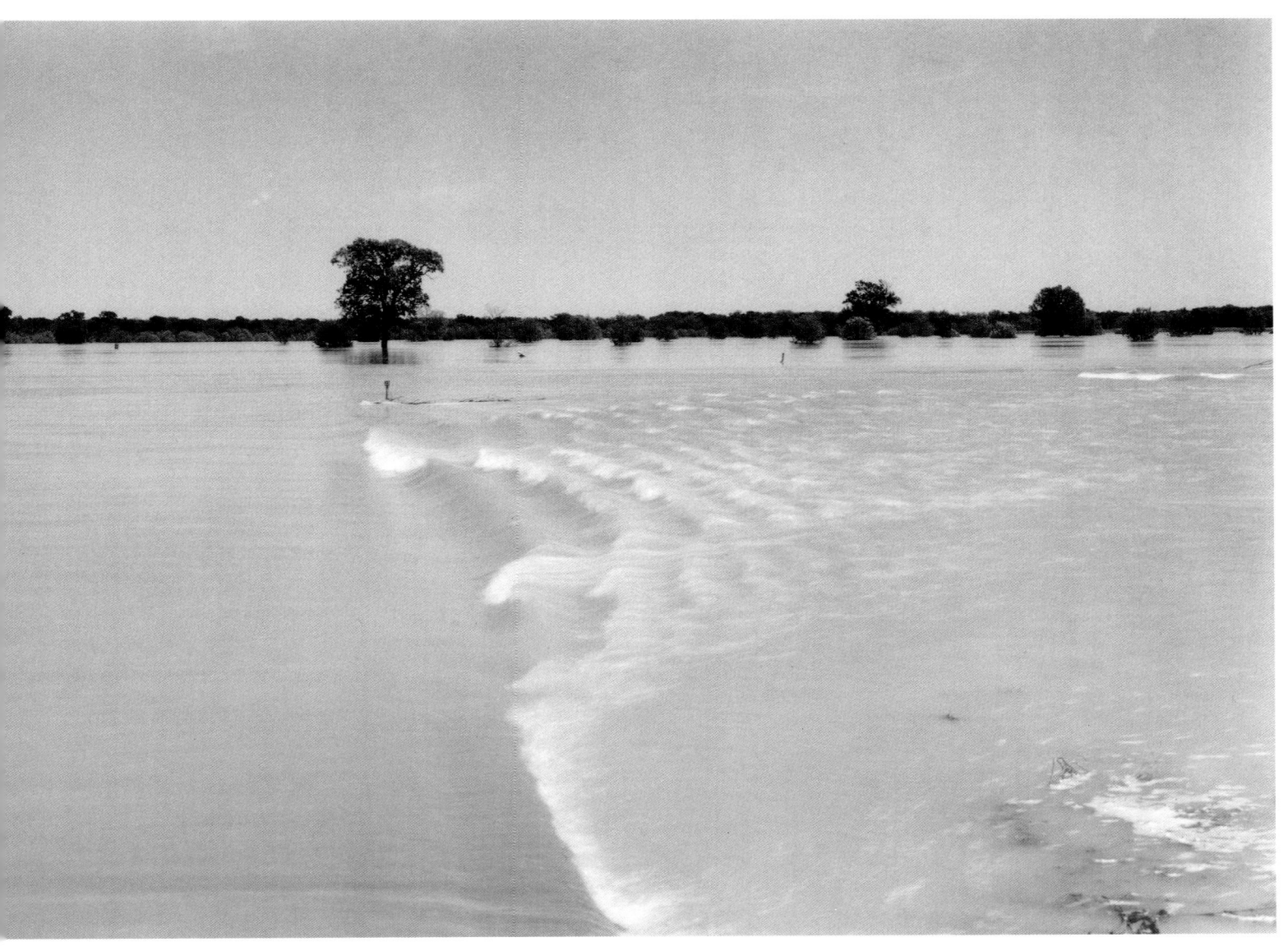

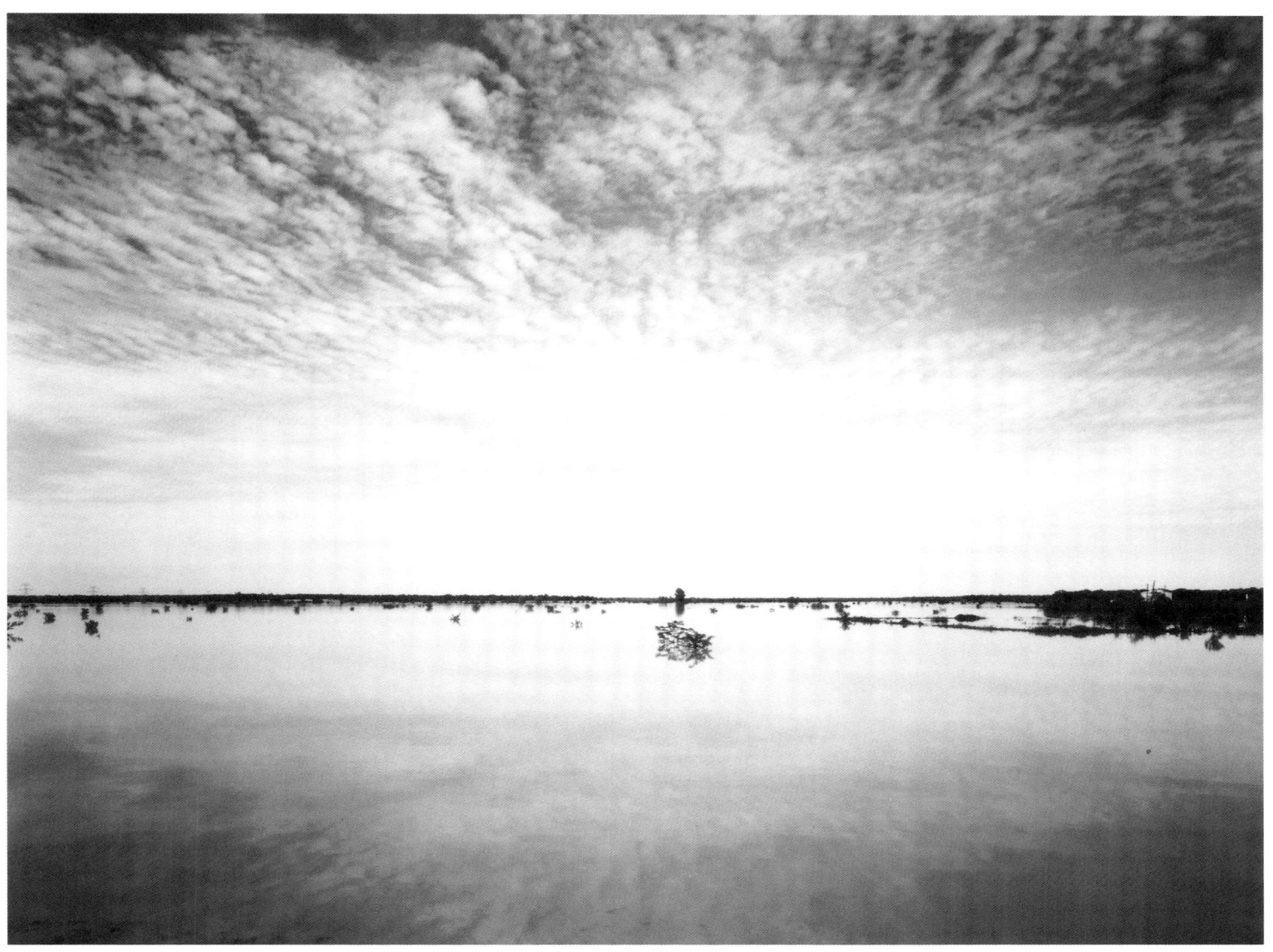

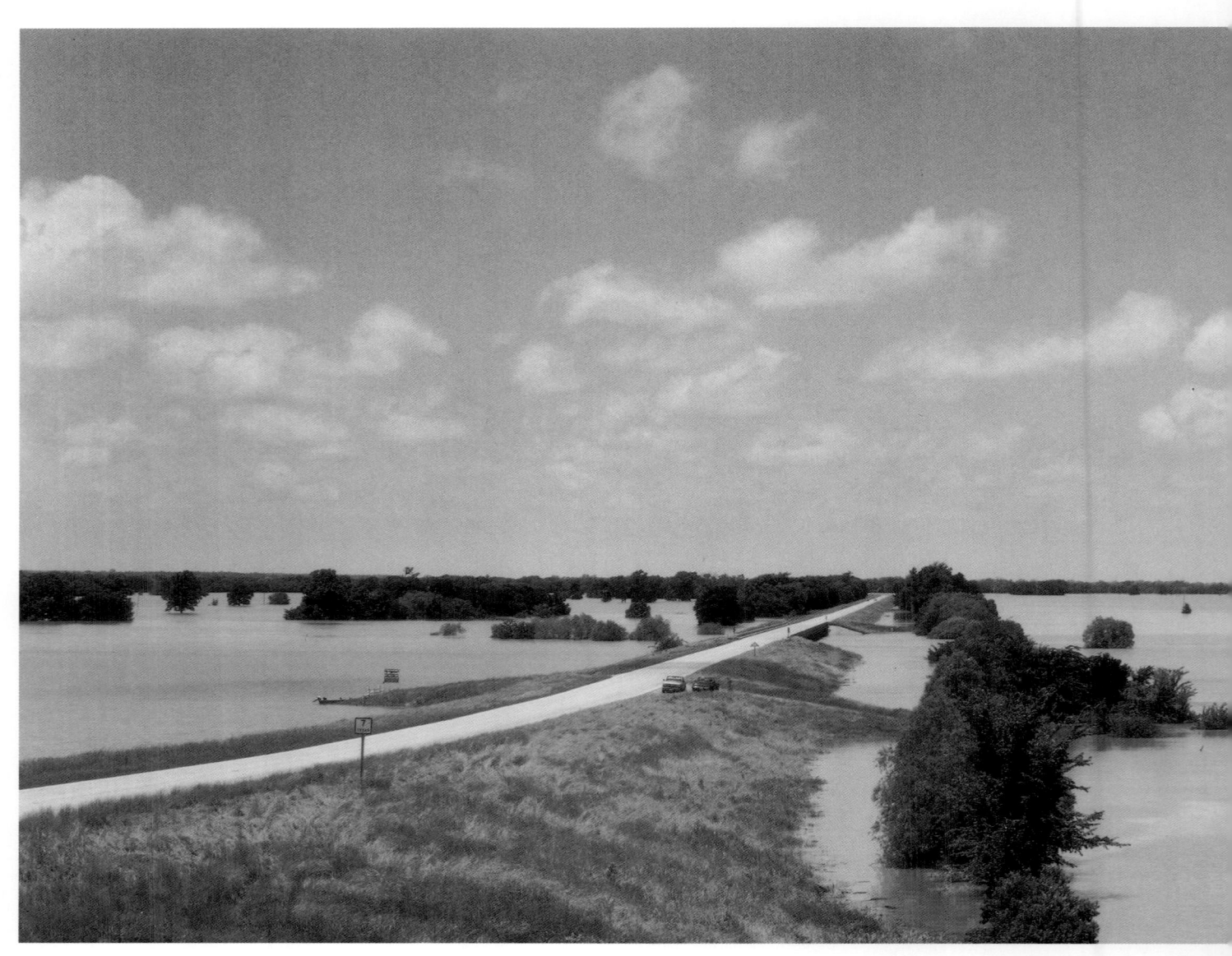

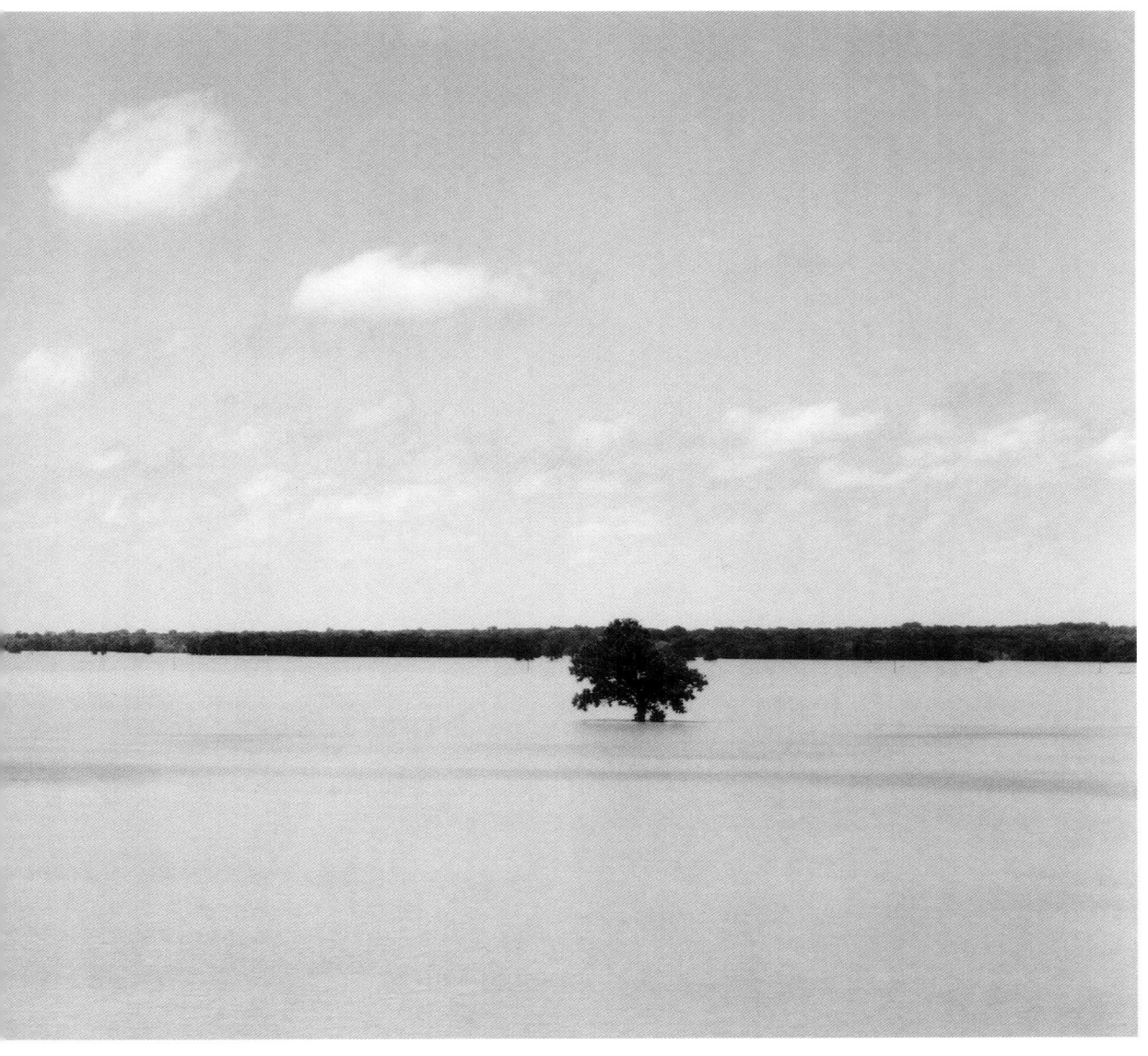

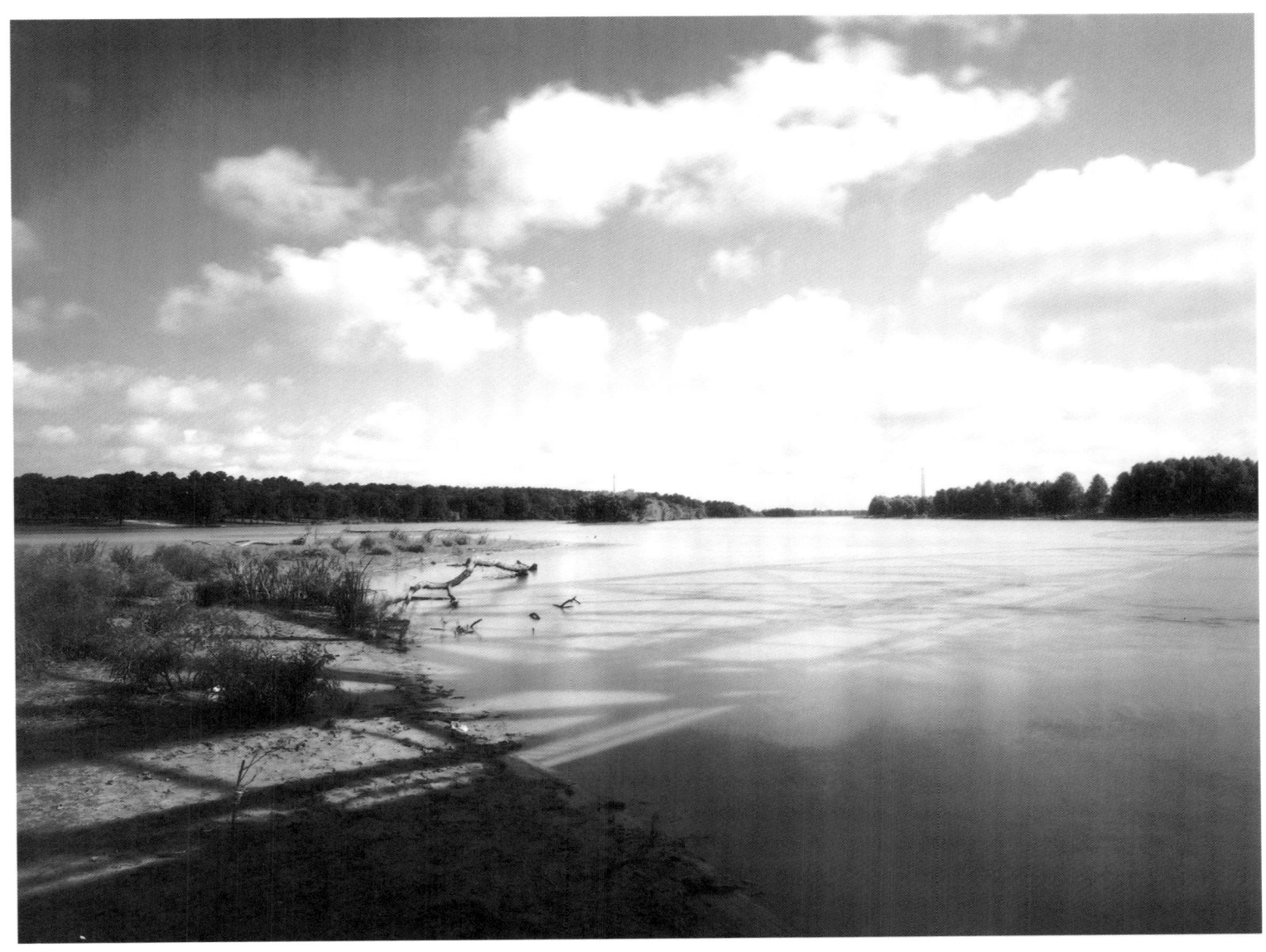

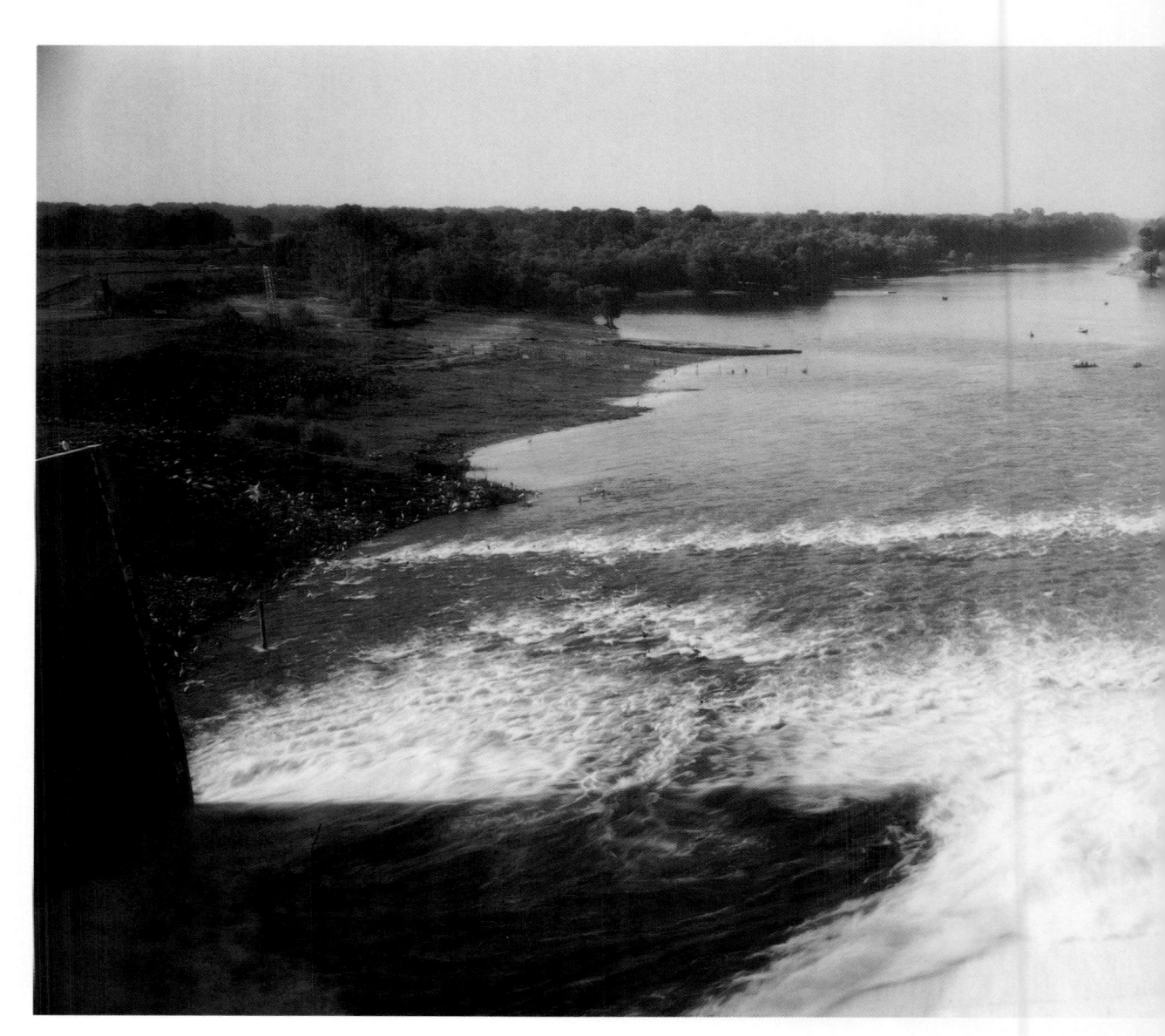

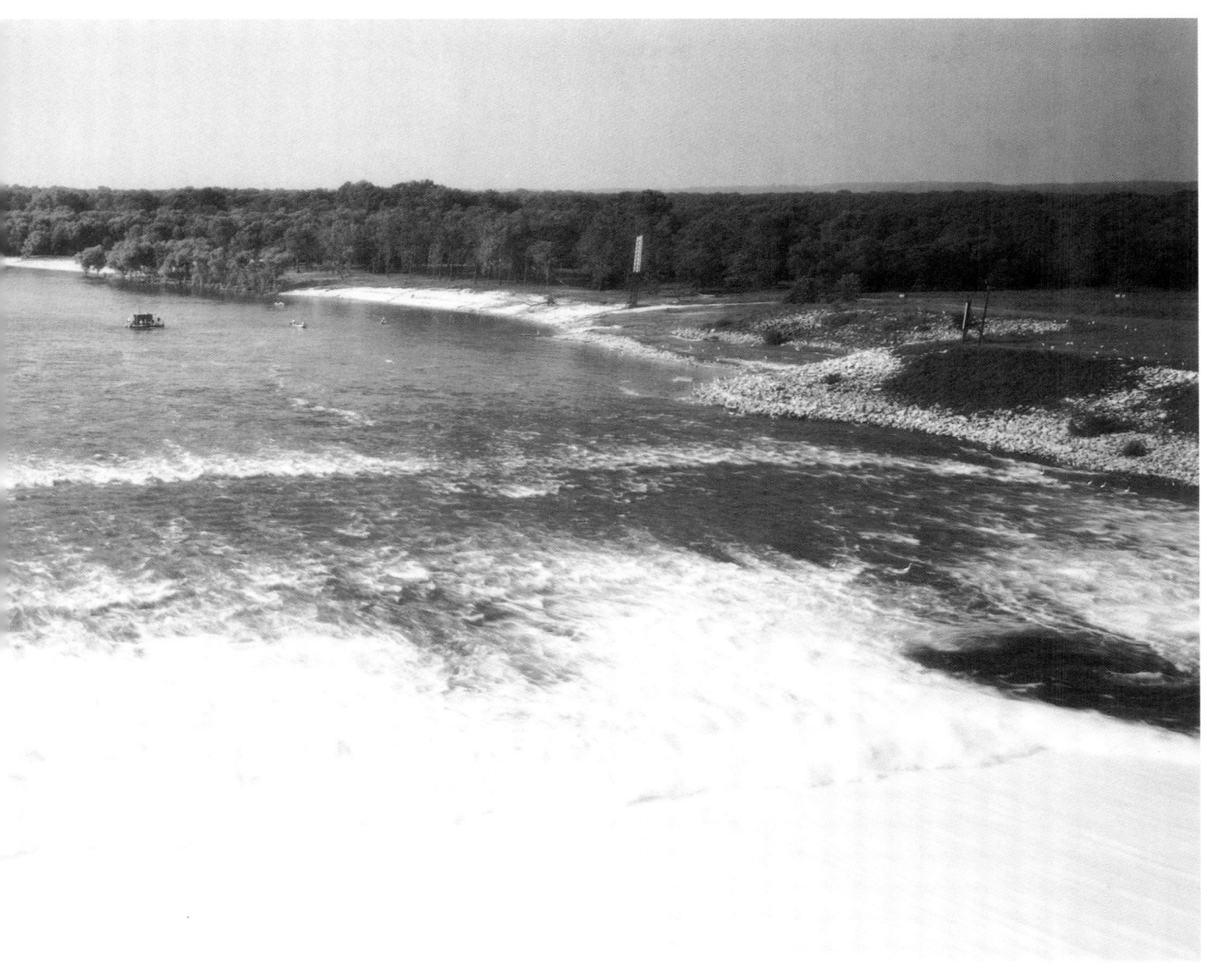

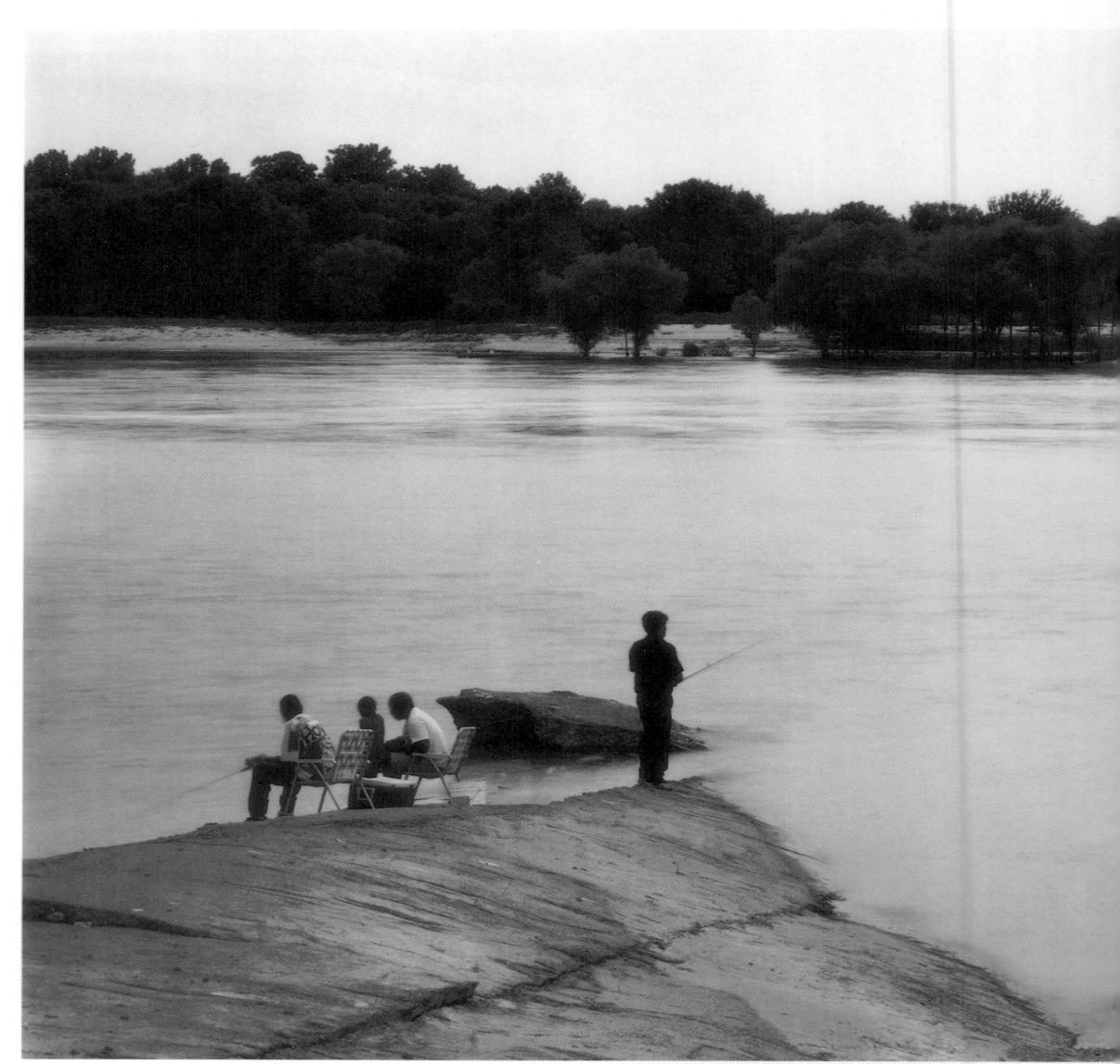

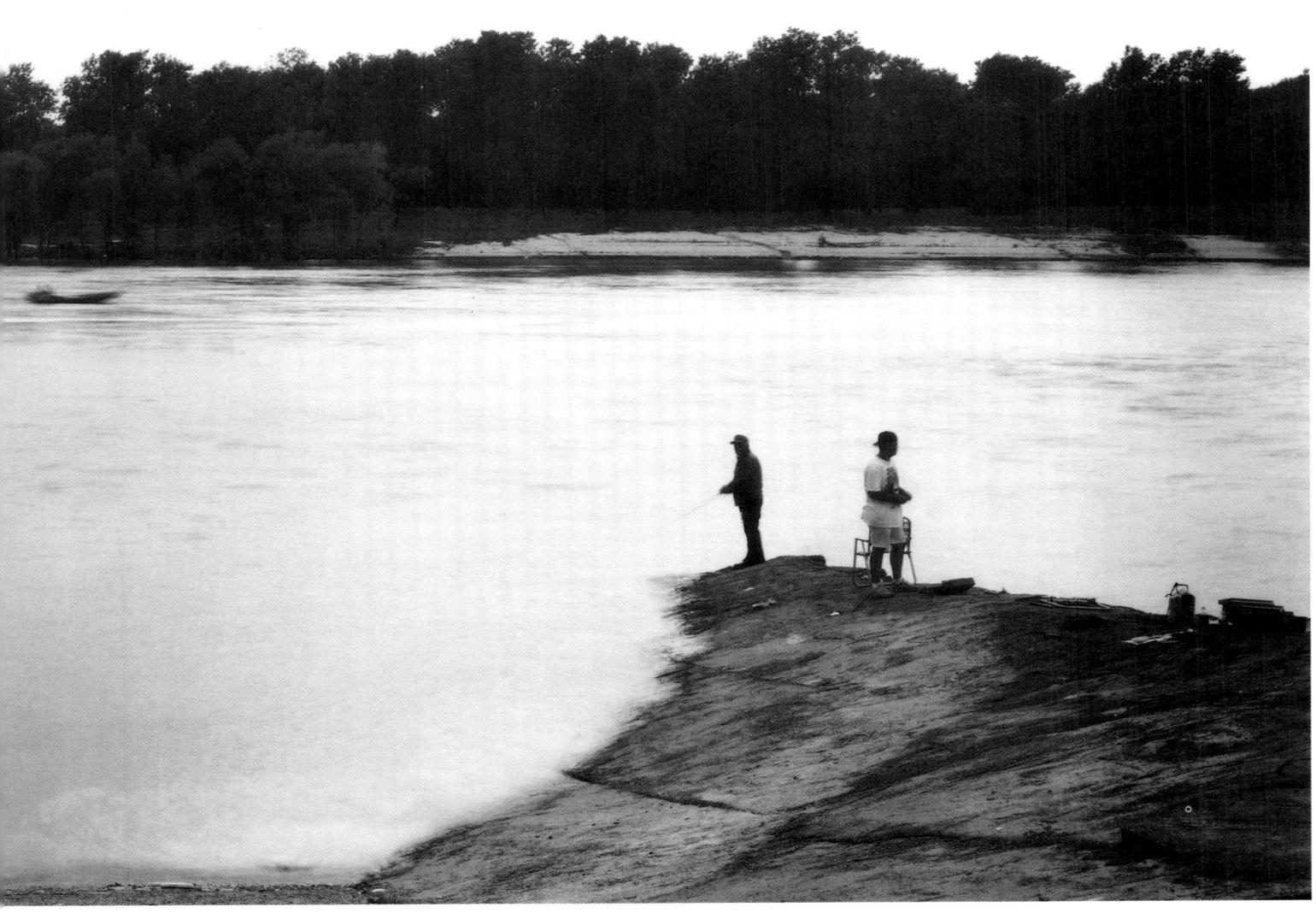

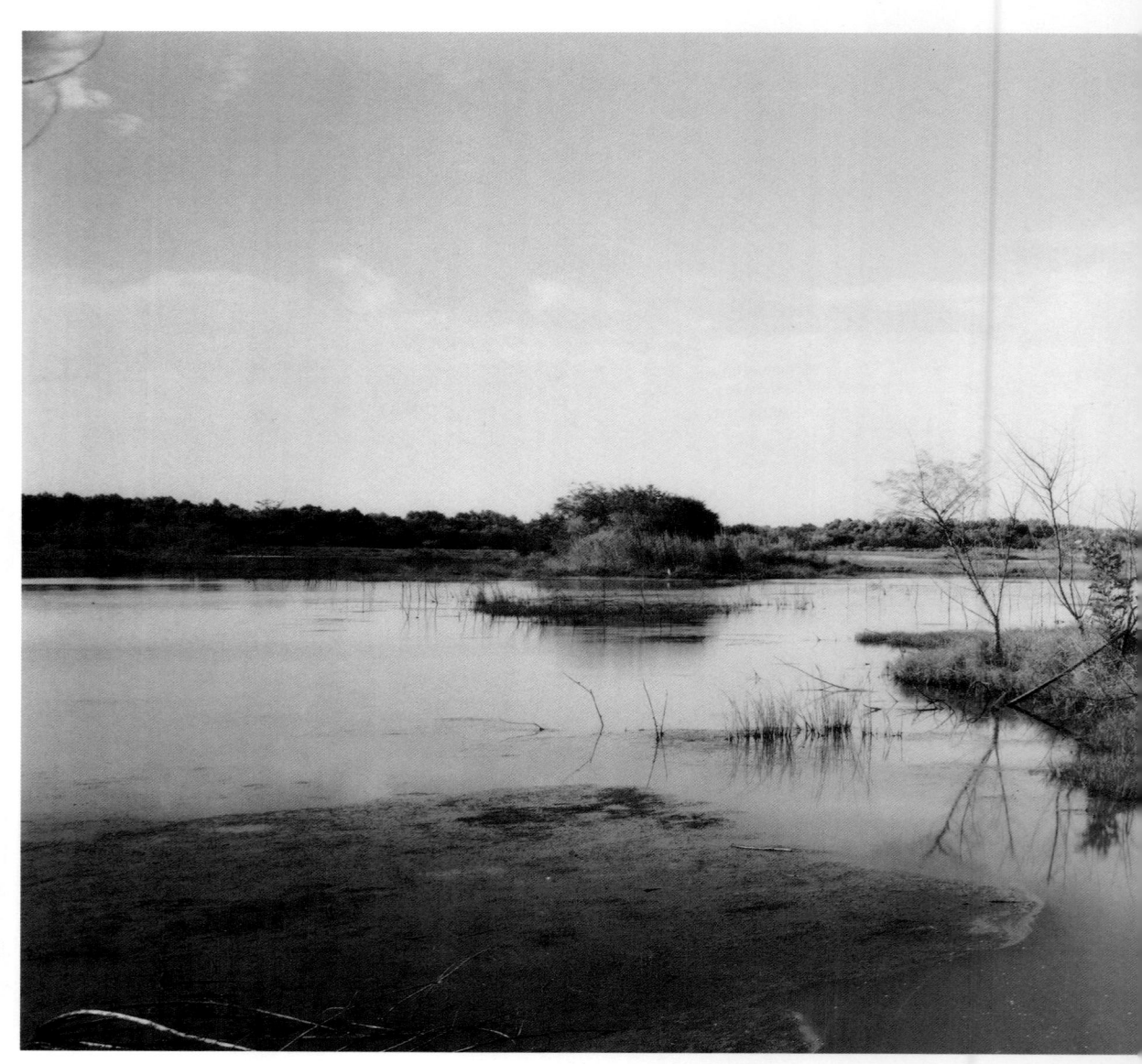

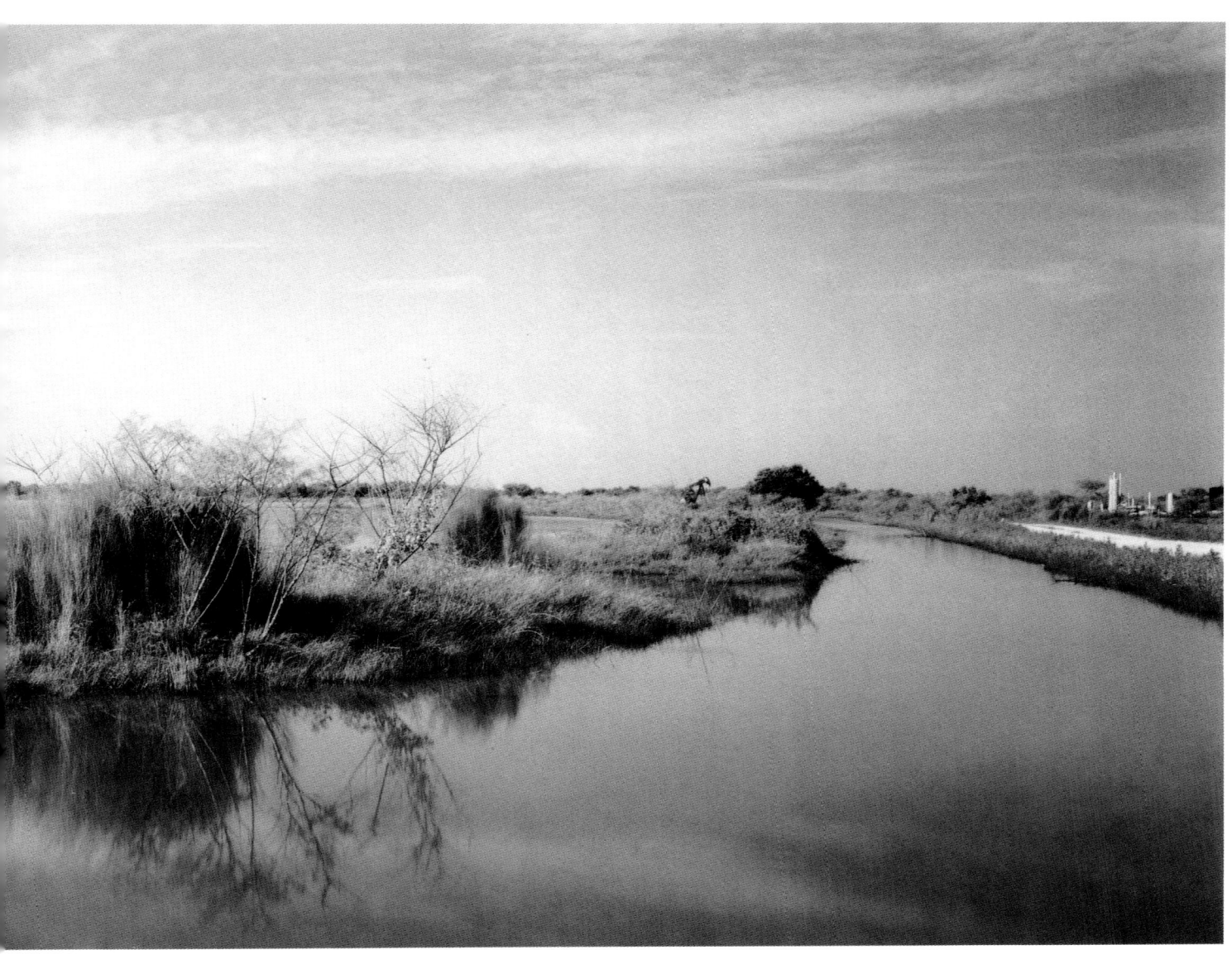

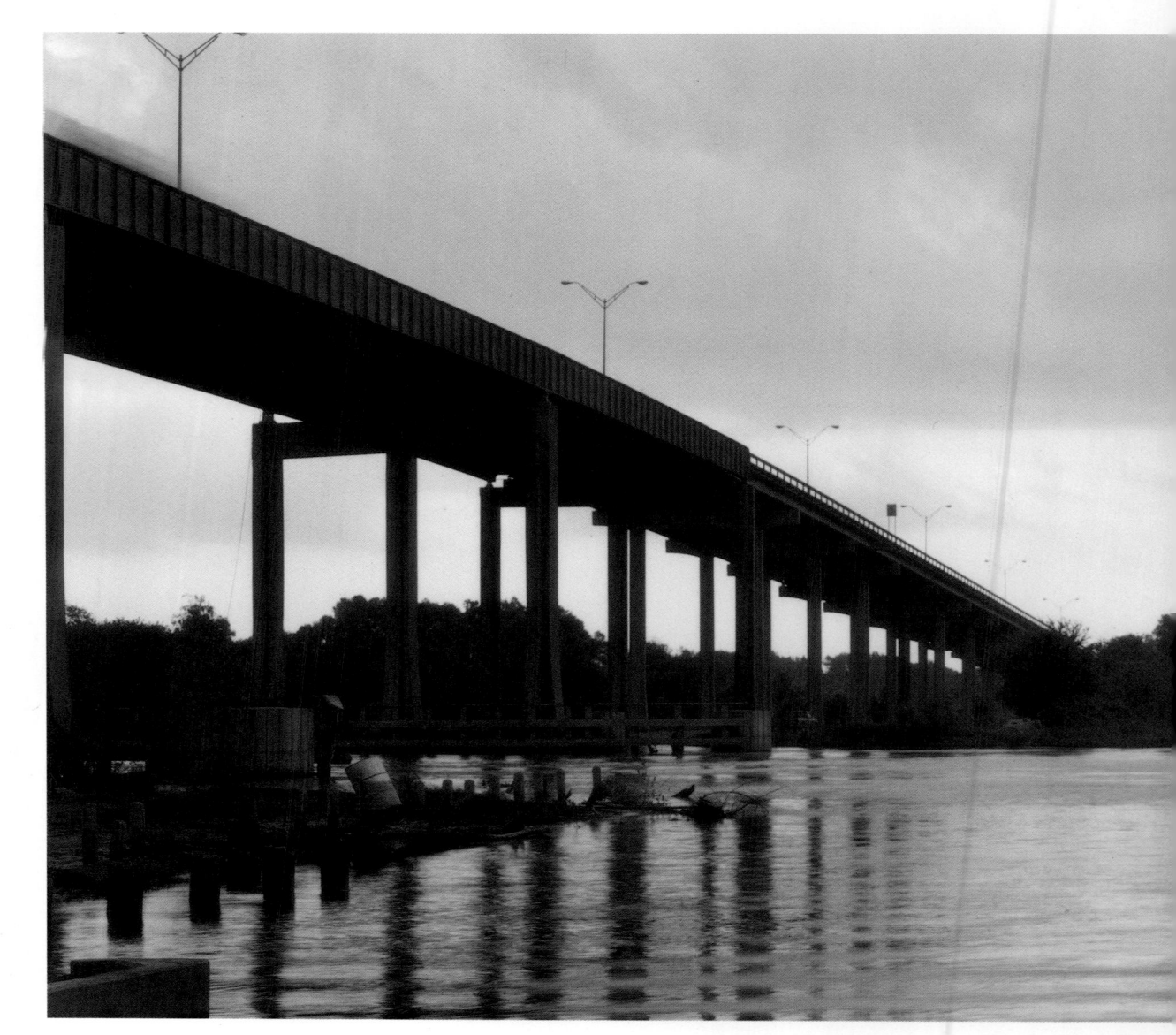

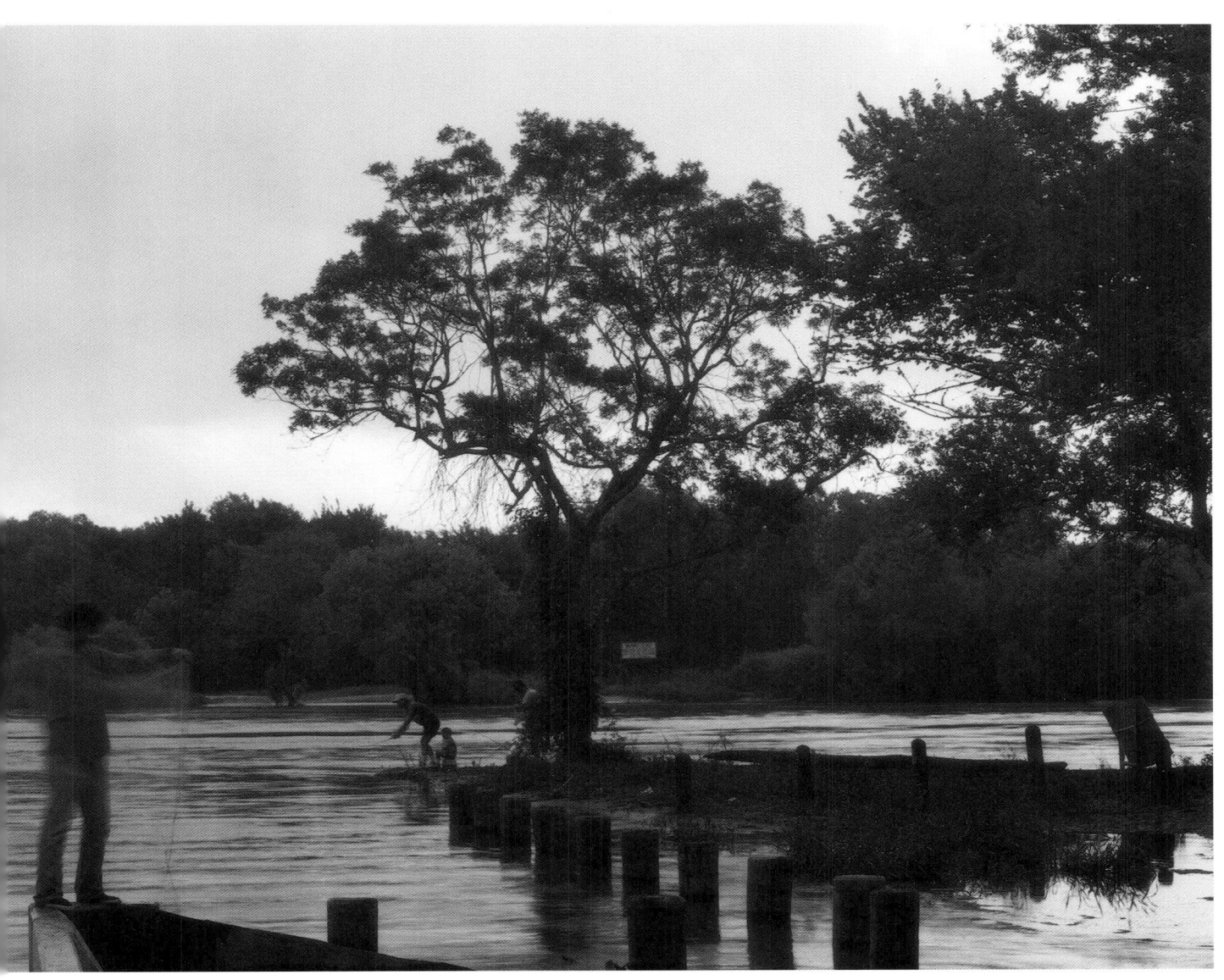

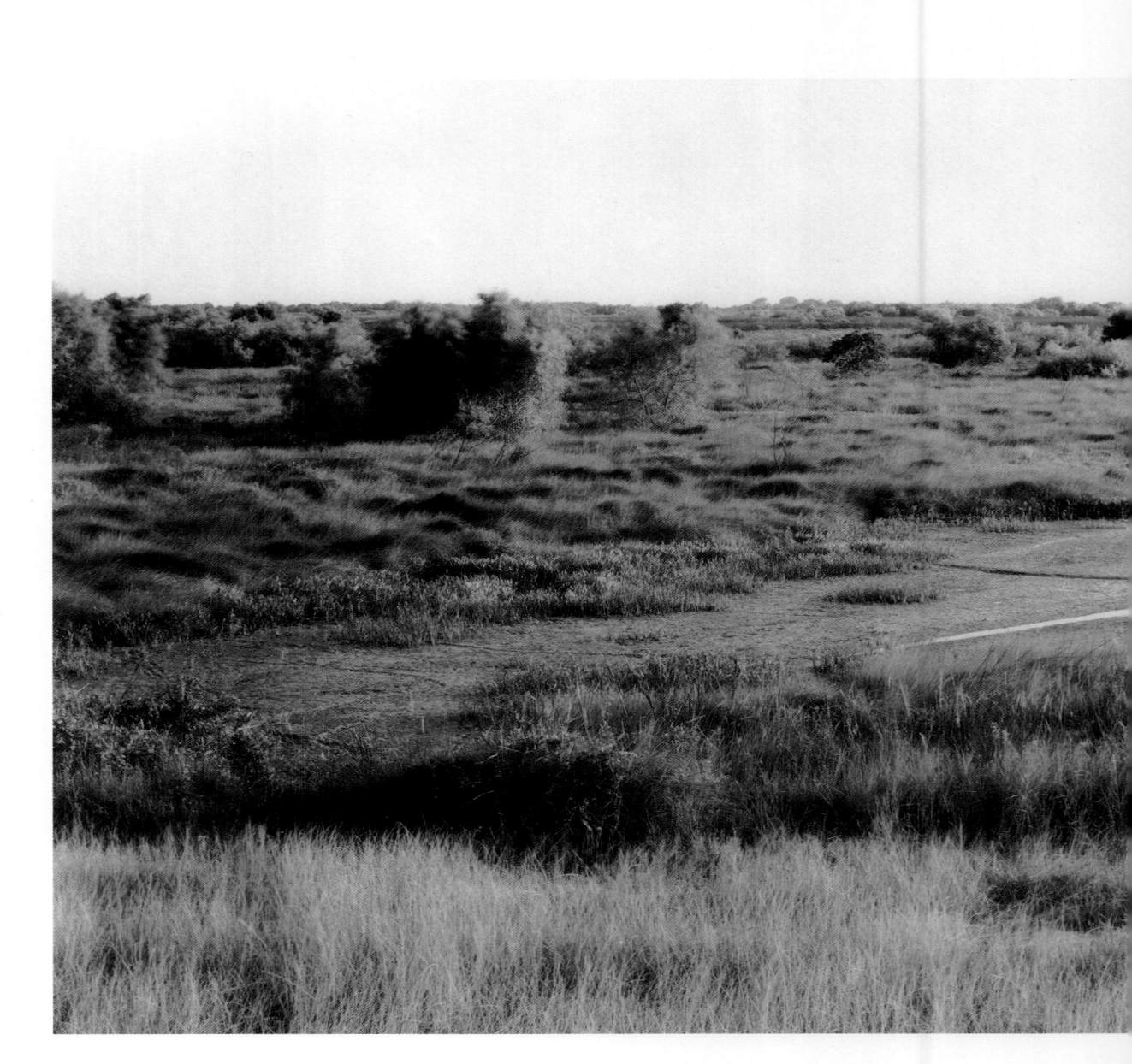

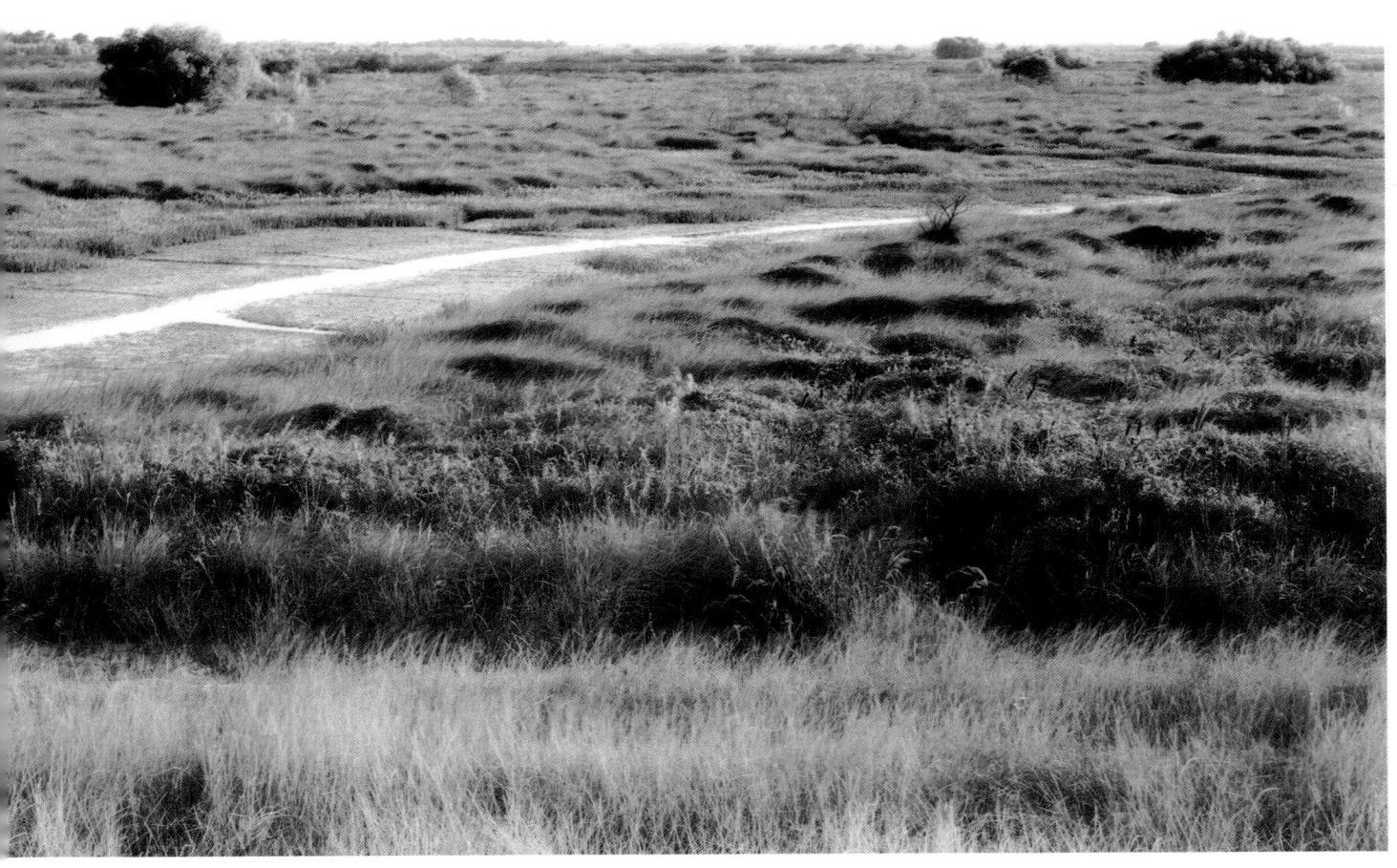

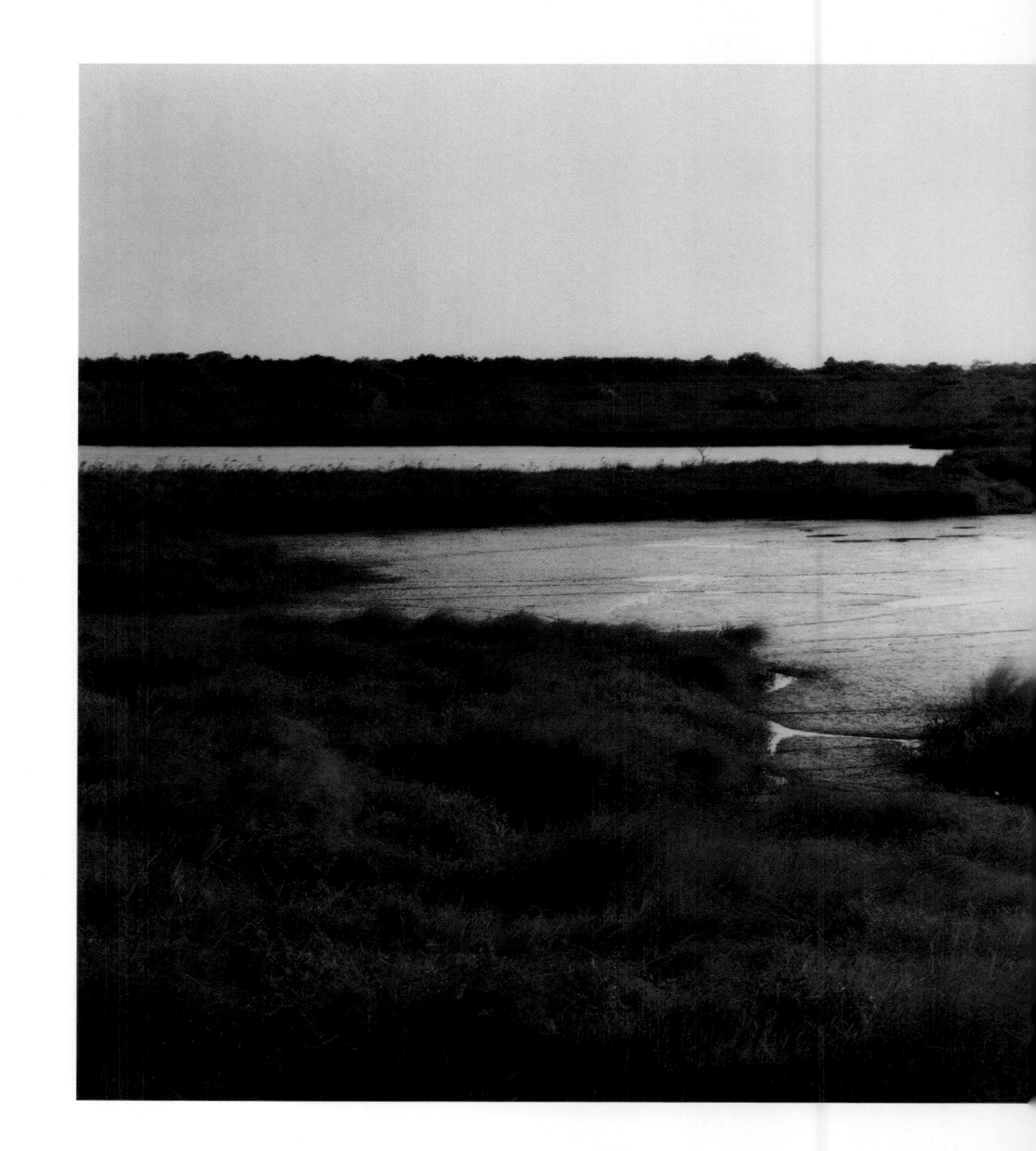

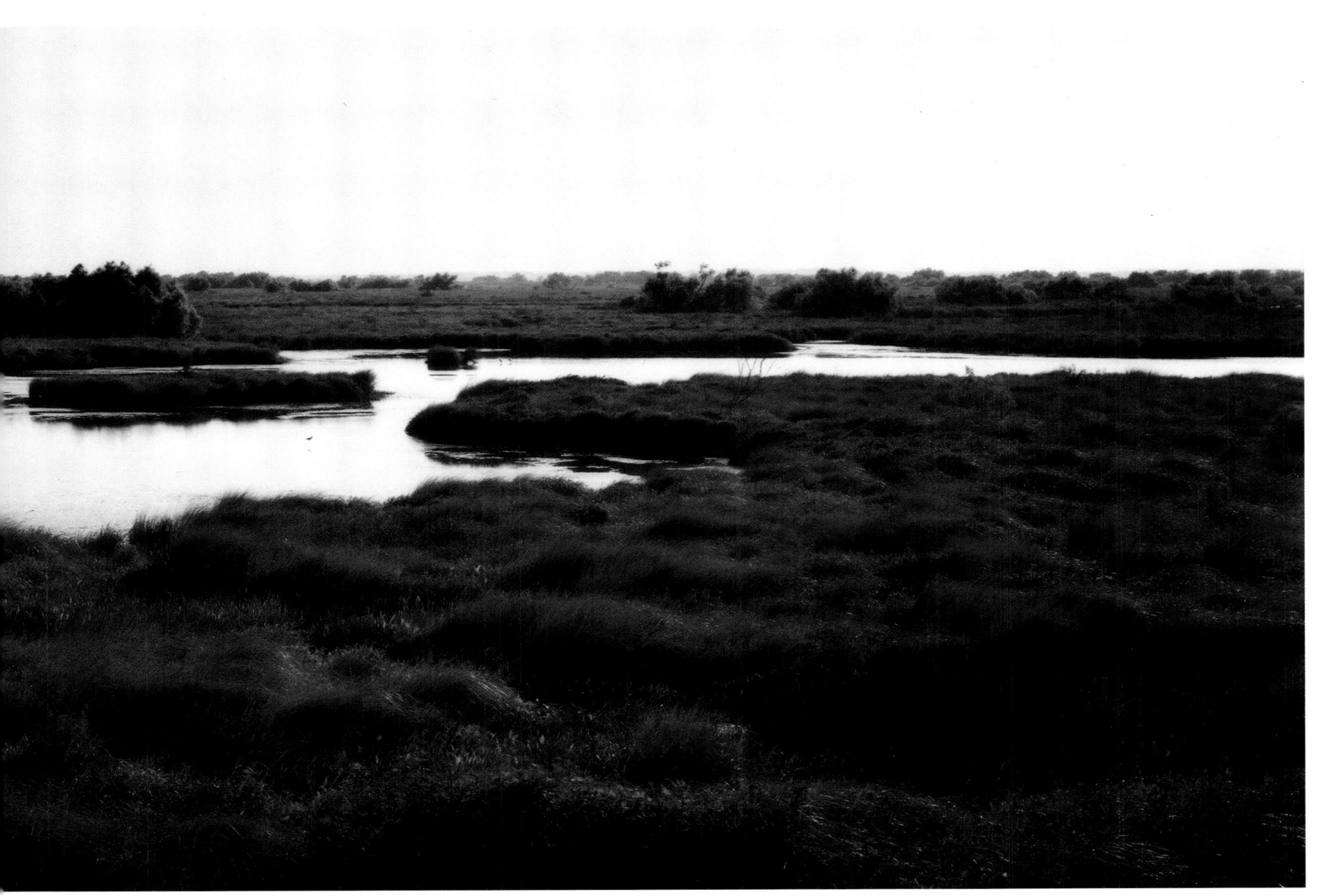

Luther Smith's notes on the photographs

1. West Fork, looking west on western edge northeast of Olney, October 24, 1990. A rain drop falling west of this point will end up in the Brazos River, a rain drop falling north of (to the right at this point) will end up in the Red River and a rain drop falling within the space of this picture will end up in the Trinity River.

2. West Fork, off McMurtry Road, Archer County, December 11, 1990. The rainfall in this western part of the Trinity averages less than thirty inches per year.

3. West Fork, off Route 16, Archer County, September 10, 1990. This photograph, taken early in the morning before sunrise, shows the West Fork in the dry season when the river often shrinks to small pools of water.

4. North Prideau Road, overlooking the West Fork, Archer County, September 10, 1990.

5. Dead tree, stock tank, south of Jacksboro, July 1986.

6. West Fork, south of Bridgeport, February 18, 1991.

7. A branch near the beginning of the Elm Fork, near Saint Jo, October 16, 1990.

8. Cooke County landscape, along the Elm Fork, south of Lindsay, December 18, 1990. This shows some of the rich, fertile soil along the banks of the Elm Fork.

9. Elm Fork, south of Gainesville, December 18, 1990. During the dry season, the trees along the river provide a canopy of shade and protect the river environment. During floods they provide obstacles for the fast-moving floodwaters. This photograph shows the effect of the floodwaters tearing loose anything not well attached.

10. Clear Fork, east of Toto, west of Union, September 1990. Of the four forks of the Trinity, the Clear Fork is the smallest, originating near Springtown and flowing into the West Fork north of downtown Fort Worth.

11. Clear Fork, off Route 51, June 8, 1994.

12. East Fork, between Weston and Anna, April 9, 1991. This area is one of the most beautiful along the Trinity. The bridge has been damaged by floods, leaving this tranquil area mostly undisturbed for many years. Now the area is rapidly developing, and in a few years this part of the river will probably be made into a ditch with cement sides so that houses and businesses built here will not be threatened by flooding.

13. East Fork, north of McKinney, February 29, 1991. This is how I imagine the river looked before European settlers arrived. The trees grow near the river because of the availability of water. When the floods come, the trees are mangled.

14. Looking upstream, East Fork, west of Melissa, November 28, 1992.

15. Trees along the East Fork, north of McKinney, December 10, 1990.

16. East Fork, north of McKinney, December 10, 1990.

17. East Fork, north of McKinney, April 9, 1991 (the same site as #16).

18. East Fork, near Melissa, October 1990. This is one of the places that convinced me that pollution is a problem that we have as individuals. Easy as it is to blame institutions for the pollution of the river, it was probably some individual who dumped these fifty-five-gallon barrels into the river.

19. East Fork, west of Melissa, December 10, 1990.

20. Stock tank off Farmer Road, west of Fort Worth, October 8, 1989.

21. Looking north off Route 380, Lake Lavon, October 1990.

22. Shoreline, Lake Ray Roberts, off Route 3002. All the impounds, stock tanks, and reservoirs on the Trinity are man-made. As this reservoir filled, it created a condition similar to a flood, because the farmland was flooded to create the lake.

23. Lake Ray Hubbard, off FM 66 near Rowlett, October 4, 1990. Lake Ray Hubbard, an early reservoir, built in 1967, is a typical lake with trees and other foliage along the bank.

24. Lake Lewisville from park, January 31, 1991. Tires found along the river serve as a reminder of the relationship between humans and the river. We use the river as a place of recreation, a water source, and a waste-disposal system. Sometimes these uses are incompatible.

25. Spillway, Benbrook Lake, June 12, 1989. This was the first time since 1957 that the river went over the spillway at Benbrook. So many people came to see it that a parking lot had to be built for their cars. Because people continued to drive into the river, at the risk of drowning, a fence was built to keep drivers from attempting the crossing.

26. West Fork, across from Rockwood Park, Fort Worth, October 23, 1992. The "nonsource pollution"—stuff just left around, including hydrocarbons from automobile exhaust and Styrofoam cups from fast food places—washes through the storm sewers into the river.

27. Dead dog at Rockwood Park, Fort Worth, April 10, 1990.

28. West Fork across from Rockwood Park, Fort Worth, October 23, 1992. This part of the Trinity in Fort Worth has not yet been channeled.

29. Looking east from University Drive at the West Fork, Fort Worth, 1992.

30. Clear Fork at Hulen Drive, Fort Worth, March 21, 1990.

31. Trinity River from Heritage Park, Fort Worth, February 7, 1993. The confluence of the Clear and West forks can be seen from this park in downtown Fort Worth.

32. At Northside Drive, Fort Worth, November 21, 1987.

33. At Northside Drive, Fort Worth, December 1, 1987. When I set the camera up to make this photograph, it was dusk and the exposure was approximately two minutes when I opened the shutter. After the film had been exposing for about one minute, I took another reading and from that the new reading indicated an exposure of several minutes, so the dogs and I went for a walk. When we got back it had been seven minutes, so I closed the shutter hoping I would get something.

34. At Northside Drive, Fort Worth, November 26, 1988.

35. From Samuels Avenue bridge, Fort Worth, 1990.

36. Off Handley-Ederville Road, Fort Worth, April 10, 1990.

37. Off Handley-Ederville Road, Fort Worth, March 18, 1990.

38. At Westmoreland Road, Dallas, January 29, 1991.

39. Trinity River greenway from the levee, Dallas, May 13, 1990. The greenway in Dallas becomes a lake during floods.

40. Looking east across the river north of Interstate 30, downtown Dallas, July 1990.

41. Trinity River greenway near Sylvan Avenue, Dallas, October 4, 1990.

42. Looking east from the levee, Dallas, November 5, 1989, north of downtown Dallas.

43. Flood over Route 34, Ellis County, May 7, 1990. The floods were so intense that the levees were allowed to fail south of Dallas to speed the exit of water out of the cities to the north.

44. Flood over U.S. Highway 287, Freestone County, May 10, 1990. U. S. Highway 287 is a major four-lane highway running diagonally from Beaumont to Amarillo. In 1990, it was temporarily closed due to flooding.

45. Flood off U. S. Highway 287, Freestone County, May 10, 1990.

46. Flood at Route 7 west of Crockett, Houston County, May 9, 1990. The river, usually measured in yards, at this point is more than three miles across.

47. Near Riverside, June 22, 1990.

48. From the Lake Livingston Dam, Polk County, July 20, 1994.

49. Fishing below Lake Livingston Dam, Polk County, July 20, 1994.

50. Old oil field, north of Interstate 10, Trinity River basin, near Wallisville, Chambers County, July 19, 1994.

51. Fisherman at Interstate 10, near Wallisville, Chambers County, June 21, 1990.

52. Marsh, south of Interstate 10, near Wallisville, Chambers County, July 18, 1994.

53. Marsh, lower Trinity basin, south of Interstate 10, near Wallisville, Chambers County, July 18, 1994. Annual rainfall in this area averages fifty-one inches, almost twice that of the upper Trinity.

Contributors

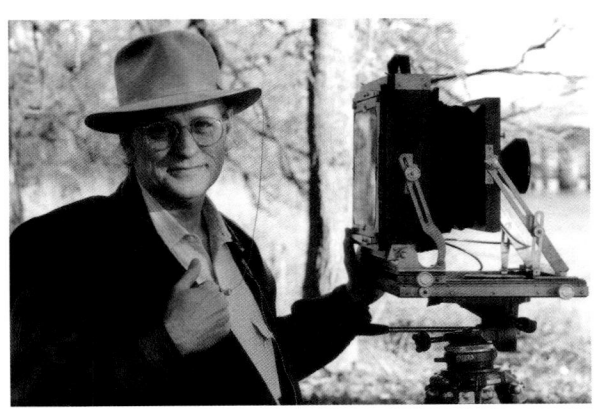 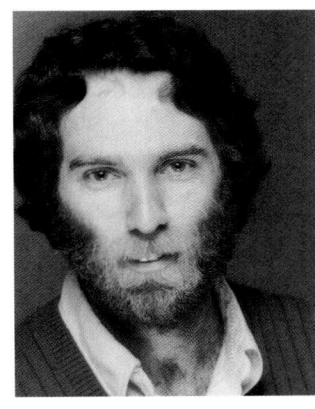 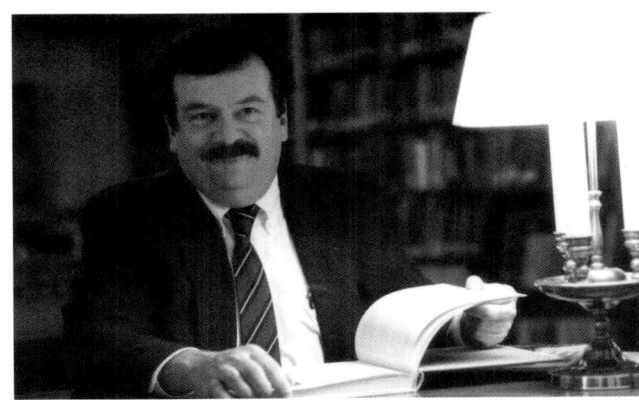

Luther Smith, professor of photography, has taught at Texas Christian University since 1983.

Mike Nichols, a free-lance writer and editor, is a former newspaper columnist and the author of three books. When it comes to the Trinity River, he knows whereof he writes—he is a lifelong resident of the Trinity basin and lives on Rock Tank Creek, a tributary of the river.

Thomas W. Southall has been professor of art history and curator of photography, Spencer Museum of Art at the University of Kansas, and curator of photography at Fort Worth's Amon Carter Museum. In 1996 he held a Joshua C. Taylor Fellowship at the National Museum of American Art, Smithsonian Institution, Washington, D.C.